BRITISH ACADEMY
OF MANAGEMENT

Management Impact
Series Editors: Jean M. Bartunek, Nic Beech and Cary Cooper

Scholarly research into business and management proliferates globally. Its impact into management practice can be difficult to monitor and measure. This series, published in association with The British Academy of Management, presents Shortform books that demonstrate how management scholarship has impacted upon the real world.

Incorporating case study examples and highlighting the link between scholarship, policy, and practice, the series provides an essential resource for postgraduate students and researchers seeking to understand how to create impact through their work. The concise nature of the books also ensures that they can be useful reading for reflective practitioners.

Delivering Impact in Management Research
When Does it Really Happen?
Robert MacIntosh, Katy Mason, Nic Beech and Jean M. Bartunek

Impact and the Management Researcher
Usha C.V. Haley

The Research Impact Agenda
Navigating the Impact of Impact
Martyna Śliwa and Neil Kellard

For more information about this series, please visit: www.routledge.com/ Management-Impact/book-series/IMPACTM

The Research Impact Agenda

Navigating the Impact of Impact

Martyna Śliwa and Neil Kellard

Routledge
Taylor & Francis Group

LONDON AND NEW YORK

First published 2022
by Routledge
2 Park Square, Milton Park, Abingdon, Oxon OX14 4RN

and by Routledge
605 Third Avenue, New York, NY 10158

Routledge is an imprint of the Taylor & Francis Group, an informa business

© 2022 Martyna Śliwa and Neil Kellard

British Library Cataloguing-in-Publication Data
A catalogue record for this book is available from the British Library

Library of Congress Cataloguing-in-Publication Data
Names: Śliwa, Martyna, author. | Kellard, Neil, author.
Title: The research impact agenda : navigating the impact of impact / Martyna Śliwa and Neil Kellard.
Description: First Edition. | New York : Routledge, 2022. | Series: Management Impact / series editors, Jean M. Bartunek, Nic Beech and Cary Cooper | Includes bibliographical references and index.
Identifiers: LCCN 2021037533 (print) | LCCN 2021037534 (ebook) | ISBN 9780367547493 (Hardback) | ISBN 9780367547516 (Paperback) | ISBN 9781003090465 (eBook)
Subjects: LCSH: Education, Higher--Research--Cross-cultural studies. | Education, Higher--Social aspects--Cross-cultural studies. | Education, Higher--Economic aspects--Cross-cultural studies. | Higher education and state--Cross-cultural studies. | Educational equalization.
Classification: LCC LB2326.3 .S55 2022 (print) | LCC LB2326.3 (ebook) | DDC 378.007--dc23
LC record available at https://lccn.loc.gov/2021037533
LC ebook record available at https://lccn.loc.gov/2021037534

ISBN: 978-0-367-54749-3 (hbk)
ISBN: 978-0-367-54751-6 (pbk)
ISBN: 978-1-003-09046-5 (ebk)

DOI: 10.4324/9781003090465

Typeset in Times New Roman
by MPS Limited, Dehradun

Contents

Introduction

This book contributes to the growing body of work addressing the processes and consequences of national governments' audits of the performance of higher education institutions (HEIs) in different countries. Specifically, we address one recent area of focus within these audits, namely the measurement of universities' societal and economic impact. Since the book is part of a collaborative 'short format' series between the British Academy of Management and Routledge dedicated to business and management research impact, central to our discussion are issues related to the generation and measurement of impact of business schools in the UK conducted as part of the Research Excellence Framework (REF) audit. However, this does not mean that the relevance of our argument is limited to the UK or, indeed, the business school context. Although audit frameworks similar to the REF have been introduced in other national higher education systems, e.g. Australia, Brazil, and Poland, the UK is the first country in which the measurement of universities' impact has taken place, and therefore the first – and so far the only – source of rich, empirical material on impact assessment that we have been able to analyse and discuss.

The ability to develop insights based on our analysis of the UK REF impact process and its multi-faceted consequences for business schools and their staff has provided us with the opportunity to put forward an argument that is valid and applicable within the international context and in relation to the whole higher education sector, in particular in those countries that are considering the inclusion of impact in future audits of universities' performance. Australia, e.g. carried out its first Engagement and Impact (EI) assessment in 2018, with the next exercise scheduled for 2024. As such, in addition to university and business school leaders and academics, as well as leaders of the two key UK-based professional associations, i.e. the

DOI: 10.4324/9781003090465-101

British Academy of Management and the Chartered Association of Business Schools, we hope that our book will be of interest to politicians and HE policymakers internationally. Moreover, accrediting and professional bodies, with business school partners around the globe including in Africa, Asia, and South America, are increasingly including positive societal impact as a measurable requirement. Above all, we have written it for everybody – regardless of their formal position, organisational affiliation, or career stage – who considers it important to reduce and remove inequalities and inequities within the HE sector and to make our universities and business schools more inclusive.

Importantly, this book is a problematisation of the impact generation and assessment agenda and has not been intended as a guide for producing a 'REF-able' impact case study. Instead, we hope it will trigger reflection in our readers whom we invite to engage in an exchange of ideas with the aim of transforming the current framing, delivery, and assessment of business and management research impact.

The remainder of the book has been divided into six chapters.

Chapter 1 addresses the historical context underpinning the evolution of universities and within them business schools as educational establishments tasked with the formation of a new cadre of managers. We point out that debates about the role of universities have a long tradition, and that from an historical perspective, the idea of universities' societal and economic usefulness, assessed by the state through a performance audit, is relatively new.

Chapter 2 offers an overview of extant literature on the impact and relevance of business and management research. In particular, it draws attention to the relative scarcity of studies addressing the complexities and practicalities of impact generation, not least with regard to the researcher–practitioner relationship. We also highlight the limitations of the literature in that it tends to exclude management education from discussions of business and management research impact.

Chapter 3 explains the current framing of research impact assessment in the UK policy context, especially as defined through the REF. Our contextualisation of the UK's REF links it to the broader *Zeitgeist* of populism and a distrust towards 'experts', including academics. In this chapter, we also compare the REF2014 and REF2021 guidance in relation to impact and discuss which types of business schools' impact are subject to the assessment exercise.

Chapter 4 focuses on the under-researched topic of the 'impact of impact', i.e. the consequences of impact generation and evaluation for those potentially and actually involved in impact activity, i.e.

business school academics. We specifically point to the inequalities and exclusions that emerge along the lines of career stage and gender, and are associated with impact activity and assessment, arguing that the introduction of impact as part of the REF audit has not been a diversity-neutral decision.

Chapter 5 expands the analysis of the consequences of impact activity and measurement over the meso-level of business schools and universities and the macro-level of society and economy at a national and international level. Whilst recognising the potential benefits of public sector organisations' accountability, we caution about the problematic consequences of the emphasis on impact generation and assessment for business schools' ability to dedicate resources to core activities, such as teaching, research, mentoring, and administration.

Chapter 6 synthesises the key arguments presented in the book and puts forward recommendations for researchers, policymakers, university and business school leaders, and individual academics. It also highlights the relevance of the many recommendations in the book for the international context.

1 The idea of university and its societal role

1.1 Introduction

We began working on this book in June 2020 in London, with the world changing in front of our eyes as a result of the COVID-19 pandemic. Our work as researchers and educators had to move online nearly overnight, and for the first time in our professional lives we had to confront questions about how, in the new and uncertain circumstances, we are going to serve our students and colleagues, our research communities, and all other stakeholders for whom we engage in academic work. Along with the changes in the immediate realities of academic life, higher education (HE) policy decisions relevant to issues that are central to the focus of this book, i.e. the impact of academic research beyond academia, have also been changing. For example, the submission deadline for the next Research Excellence Framework (REF) audit in the UK has been postponed until March 2021. It is still uncertain how the generation of impact in the current REF period has been affected by the pandemic, and how the actual assessment of impact is going to reflect the unprecedented events of the past few months. Obviously, with the rapidly transforming world, the context of our thinking about impact has changed; what is more, since we have been witnessing how quickly priorities can shift in social, political, and economic terms, we have also been sensitised to the significance of context for our perceptions of why and how academic work matters. A reflection upon 'context', therefore, offers a helpful point of departure for our discussion of impact. We begin with contextualising the subject of academic research impact against the background of the evolution of broader debates about the societal role of universities, the rise of university-based management education, and the understanding of how, contemporarily, universities impact the society and economy.

DOI: 10.4324/9781003090465-1

1.2 An historical understanding of the societal role of universities

We locate our consideration of impact within a long-standing debate about the role of universities, which can be traced back to the ideas underpinning Wilhelm von Humboldt's reforms in 19th century Prussia. The Humboldtian model of university was first implemented with the establishment of the University of Berlin in 1810. This model came to dominate European higher education for more than a hundred years, and served as the conceptual basis of the foundation of North American research universities. The institutional formula behind the Humboldtian idea of university was developed in response to what Humboldt – whose formal position in the Prussian government was Undersecretary of State – and those surrounding him, considered a key political problem of the time:

> How is it possible to construct and then secure the necessary autonomous institutional order, or framework, to modern science and the pursuit of qualified knowledge and, at the same time, prevent it from being corrupted or even destroyed by other mighty and legitimate forces in society such as politics, economy, and religion? (Nybom, 2003: 143)

Humboldt's vision made it clear that universities should be autonomous in determining their own priorities and activities. Rather than limiting their autonomy, the obligation of the state was to protect it, and to promote 'higher learning' (*Bildung*), which was seen as central to the creation of national culture. Similarly, independence from external influences and an intellectual freedom to pursue truth-seeking and learning were considered as necessary conditions for ensuring universities' relevance to the state and the society. Humboldt himself believed that protecting the autonomy of universities was ultimately in the state's and monarch's interest. Most of all, however, his idea of university was rooted in the conviction 'that science and "virtue" (*Sittlichkeit*) could only prosper and reach its highest potential outside, and preferably above, the real political world' (Nybom, 2003: 16). As a consequence of framing the pursuit of truth-seeking as virtue, those engaging in it were also to be given autonomy and freedom to do this, whilst at the same time not being involved in any activity that directly related to political or societal matters. Inherent in Humboldt's model of university was also the conflation of research and education, with the former given primacy over the latter. Humboldt, moreover, envisaged a hierarchy of university subjects, with philosophy – and later also history – fulfilling a 'supervisory' role over more applied disciplines of knowledge: medicine, technology, and law. At the top of this hierarchy was philosophy; as a subject seen to be directly concerned with truth, it was attributed the highest value. The remaining disciplines, as associated with usefulness, were considered to be less 'noble' pursuits.

The establishment of the Humboldtian model of university resulted, throughout the 19th century, in the gradual ascent of the university – at the expense of the church – to the status of the most influential cultural and intellectual institution within the state not only in Germany but also in other European countries as well as North America. In addition, Humboldt's ideas exerted influence on thinking about the role of universities in other countries. Specifically, in the UK context, the scholarly and public debates about the purpose of higher education began with the publication, in the mid-19th century, of John Newman's *The Idea of a University Defined and Illustrated*. Echoing Humboldt's arguments, Newman's thesis rested on the assumption that the key preoccupation of universities ought to be the pursuit of knowledge for its own sake. This, to Newman, did not mean that knowledge should be generated in the form of pure research but that – along with moral and religious training – it should form part of a person's education. Central to fulfilling this idea of university as a place of the search for truth was, following Newman's own experience as a college tutor at Oxford (Anderson, 2010), the close pastoral teacher – student relationship. Underpinning the ideal of a union of teaching and research was the assumption that both teachers and students were to engage in the task of preserving and updating the existing body of theory and knowledge. Importantly, Newman's views about the role of university were closely linked to his belief in the superiority of 'universal knowledge' over any specific, specialised type of training. Universities' key task was to offer general education, with an emphasis on broad, non-vocational training of the mind, in areas such as pure sciences or the arts. This understanding of the role of universities did not include subjects of technical or vocational nature.

Both Humboldt's and Newman's ideas about universities' autonomy extended over the governance of universities, which was not expected to be subject to external mechanisms of accountability. Rather, according to the dominant perception, universities' right to self-governance constituted a necessary and positive 'force which enables universities to appoint academic staff without external interference, decide whom to admit as students, identify what they should teach and how it should be taught, control their own standards, establish their own academic priorities and determine internally their patterns of future development' (Farrant, 1987: 48). In other words, an understanding of universities commensurate with Humboldt's and Newman's ideas implied a clear boundary between the state and the universities, with the former given the role to provide funding and to ensure and protect the autonomy of the latter.

Remembering Humboldt's and Newman's influential contributions to our understanding of the purpose of universities is relevant to the current discussion of impact in the context of contemporary business schools for two reasons: 1) it demonstrates that an approach to thinking about universities through the lens of evaluating their contribution against a set of utilitarian criteria concerned with their direct 'usefulness' to society and economy, as determined by the state's authorities, need not be taken for granted. Whilst not an entirely new approach, it stands in contrast to the 19th century ideal of university as an autonomous institution dedicated to pursuit of knowledge for knowledge's sake; 2) it also highlights that academic disciplines represented in research and scholarship conducted within business schools would not have been seen as part of universities' work at the time of these early debates about the purpose of universities, and of the implementation of the Humboldtian model of higher education. In the next section, following from this background to the 19th century 'idea of the university', we discuss in more detail the evolution of thinking about universities' societal role in the 20th century towards a more utilitarian view. Within this context, we then elaborate on the inclusion of business schools within universities.

1.3 A new role of universities in the era of HE expansion

Universities in the UK, as well as across the whole of Europe, were transformed in the first half of the twentieth century. The adoption of the Humboldtian model, coupled with the prioritisation of science pursued according to the principles of logical positivism, initially meant that intellectual pursuit and the development of scientific knowledge became the main rationales underpinning higher education (Bourner, 2012). At the same time, new educational institutions – such as technical colleges and research institutes – were being created with a remit to engage in 'applied' education and research, to serve the requirements of industrial society. Coupled with this, a new trend emerged towards opening the traditionally elite system of HE to groups previously excluded. This democratisation of university education was underpinned by two phenomena. First, industrialisation brought with it the need for educated and well-trained 'talent', whereas broader social change, represented and accomplished by both feminist and working class movements meant that members of groups previously practically absent from university education were now in the position to execute their right to participate in it (Perkin, 2007). Widening access to HE was a particularly visible phenomenon in England, where – as a consequence of the introduction of state-funded scholarships – the proportion of working-class students increased from 1% to 29% between 1910 and 1930 (Kaelble, 1985). Further, as Perkin (2007) notes, women began to be allowed to participate in HE: first, through joining women's colleges founded in the second half of the 19th century, and second, through being admitted to universities. Worth noting is that it was not until 1920 and 1948 that the universities of Oxford and Cambridge, respectively, formally accepted women as full university members.

With more students from minority and disadvantaged backgrounds entering HE, the training provided by universities gradually gained a more vocational and applied profile. In particular, after World War II, HE experienced intensive expansion across the world, with existing universities increasing in size and new universities being founded. In particular, in the global North, where the HE sector was already well established, the increase in the proportion of people undertaking university education in the second half of the 20th century was especially striking: in the UK, it grew between 1960 and 2000 from less than 10% to 60%; in Germany from 6% to 54%; and in the USA from 32% to 81% (Perkin, 2007). At the same time, the model of HE was ceasing to reflect Humboldtian ideals of 'higher learning' pursued independently of external influences and pressures from the 'real political world'. On the contrary, the HE sector was evolving in response to the socioeconomic need for managers and employees who would be both knowledgeable and capable of applying specialised knowledge from a variety of disciplines, from traditional ones such as medicine and law, to more recently developing ones such as computer science and management.

In the UK, the beginning of a shift away from an emphasis on universities' autonomy and towards accountability in relation to evaluating their societal role was marked by the 1946 changes to the University Grant Committee's (UGC) – first established in 1911 – terms of reference:

> To assist, in consultation with the universities and other bodies concerned, the preparation and execution of such plans for the

development of the universities as may from time to time be required in order that they are fully adequate to national needs (quoted in Tapper and Salter, 1995: 62).

This re-articulation of the UGC's role, for the first time made explicit the government's expectation that in their work, British universities should be driven by the objective of meeting 'national needs'. Whilst the UGC's terms of reference did not define what specifically the term 'national needs' referred to, there was no mention of pursuit of knowledge for its own sake. The financial reliance of the universities on the state, operationalised in the acceptance of funds granted by the UGC, was beginning to give shape to a new understanding of the place of universities within society. Nevertheless, as Tapper and Salter (1995) point out, in the first decades after World War II, the links between government and the universities maintained to a large extent personal, rather than purely formal or bureaucratic character, due to the existence of an 'élite consensus' about the traditional purpose of a university. However, the economic crisis of the mid-1970s resulted in cuts to the amount of the recurrent UGC grant to universities, and an evolution of the relationship between the state and the universities in the direction of stricter state control. This control took the form of the introduction of research evaluation exercises (RAEs), the first of which took place in 1986, as a mechanism to determine the amount of funding allocated to universities (Bence and Oppenheim, 2005). In addition, the government began to influence 'the academic map of higher education' (Tapper and Salter, 1995: 65) through its policy of making resources available for the expansion of programmes which it wished to grow. These programmes were primarily of an applied nature, such as technology and engineering. As a result, universities were directed to grow in a way that government believed would support the country's economic development.

Arguably, relative to the past, the 20thcentury brought a transformation from aristocratic to meritocratic society, at least in the so-called developed countries (McConnell et al., 1973). The transition of higher education from 'elite' to 'mass' was part of that transformation. Importantly, this more inclusive system, which presented social mobility opportunities for those from lower social classes as well as women, was now also given a different role by the state. Rather than benefitting from the state's protection of their autonomy and an independent pursuit of research and education, universities became subjected to expectations to prove themselves to be socially and economically useful. These demands for accountability emerged given a large, inclusive HE sector required a much greater amount of funding than a smaller elite version. In those countries where universities are primarily funded via general taxation, they are a significant item within the country's public education budget. On the other hand, where participation in HE is financed predominantly by the students and their families, accessing it constitutes a significant individual expense. Regardless of the universities' financing model in a given country, the expansion of public HE resulted in greater involvement of the state – through a system of teaching- and research-related standards, audits, and reporting requirements – in the functioning of universities. At the same time, calls on universities to demonstrate their 'value for money' and 'relevance' replaced the previously unquestioned status of universities as autonomously self-governed 'ivory towers'. It is within this context of the democratisation and growth of higher education, coupled with a changing place of universities in society, that university-based business and management education emerged.

1.4 The rise of university-based business and management education

In the UK context, the development of university-based business and management education can be traced back to the report published by the Committee on Higher Education, widely known as the 'Robbins Report', in 1963 (Larson, 2020). The report marked the beginning of a new era in UK's HE, one that would be characterised by unprecedented expansion of the university sector, in line with the 'Robbins Principle' which was originally articulated in the document, stipulating that university education should be publicly funded and available to students from all social backgrounds, as long as they 'were qualified (…) by ability and attainment' (Great Britain: Committee on Higher Education, 1963: 8). Reflecting pro-meritocracy–oriented changes across the British culture, including the business culture, the report provided foundations for widening participation (WP) in HE and the strengthening of universities' role as vehicles for social mobility. It also led to the creation of a polytechnic sector of non-university HE. Soon after the report was published, it resulted in tangible consequences for university-based business and management education, as the first two business schools in the country – London Graduate School of Business (part of the University of London) and University of Manchester Business School – 'loosely modelled after American examples' (Larson, 2020: 2) opened in the academic year 1965–66. Over the next two decades, business schools were created in many other higher education institutions (HEIs), turning university-based business and management education into the dominant form of business education (Wilson and Thomson, 2006). According to Larson (2020: 2), underpinning the expansion of business education in the post-WWII era was the intention to educate a new breed of managers who would be 'responsible corporate citizens acting both for shareholders but also with the greater needs of society in mind'. These new managers were to be trained in a variety of institutions, ranging from the most prestigious, 'flagship' postgraduate business schools and business schools based in less renowned universities and polytechnics, to further education colleges as well as privately owned organisations, be it educational providers or companies training their own managers in-house.

Both the London Graduate Business School and University of Manchester Business School quickly became the 'standard setters' for the rest of business education in the country. Placed at the top of the national hierarchy of business and management education, they offered advanced, postgraduate, and post work experience management programmes. The key objective underpinning their creation – and the subsequent proliferation and growth of business schools in Britain – was to generate improvements in the performance of British management to match the quality of management in Western Europe and North America, but also to increase the social status and respectability of British managers and of management as a career choice. Since traditionally, in the UK, managers did not enjoy a high social standing, it was understood that the manager's occupation did not attract the strongest graduates to join British companies (Vane, 1958; Kipping, 1972). By contrast, US business schools were seen to train particularly talented students, as argued in *The Statist* (1963): 'America's highly developed schools of business are turning out first-class management material, and from the best of these schools the graduates emerge with both a *broad education* and a *"professional attitude to management"'*. The drive to grow business and management education exemplified the UK government's keenness to create a new image of a manager in a manner that would help make management an attractive career option for talented graduates and, as a consequence of the application of managerial talent in business practice, increase the productivity of British business. More generally, the commissioning of a report outlining the priorities for UK higher education from Lord Robbins who himself was an economist, previously holding an academic position at the London School of Economics, symbolised the government's belief in a link between the state of HE and the country's economic growth (King and Nash, 2001). For management education, especially as far as educating prospective senior managers was concerned, an approach beneficial to fulfilling society's needs was considered to involve a breadth of knowledge, in order to ensure that managers would be able to 'strengthen the firm's performance [and] represent the firm more effectively outside the organization' (Larson, 2020: 11).

From the outset, the government's intentions to improve management practice and thus British companies' performance through developing management education by making it part of a university education, were met with ambivalence by the universities themselves. This ambivalence – or even a reluctance to include management education in university curriculum – stemmed from the view of management as 1) entirely vocational (and therefore not of relevance as a university subject) and 2) not underpinned by a body of knowledge distinct from ideas developed either in engineering or in the social sciences (Sanderson, 1972). Although there was an agreement that 'real-world', practical business problems existed and required solutions, back in the 1950s and 1960s it was not clear within which discipline these solutions could be generated, and management as well as management education were not considered to be domains that would deal with inventing and implementing these solutions, and training others in their application. In addition, universities traditionally viewed businesses, such as manufacturing, with suspicion and distrust, due to the former's presumed inadequacy in equipping graduates with skills useful in the 'business world' and the latter's profit motive (Keeble, 1992). In the early 1960s Britain, there was a wide-spread belief that businesses 'do not want to recruit graduates with first degrees in business management; they prefer a graduate with a broader education whom they can subsequently train for management either within their businesses or in postgraduate study in the universities and college or both' (NA, ED 188/155, 1962, cited in Larson, 2020). In the context of mutual biases, unsurprisingly, the expansion of university-based business management began in an environment characterised by a divide between academia and business.

Nevertheless, following the Robbins Report, this expansion took place, underpinned by the view that it provided a necessary vehicle for strengthening the country's wealth and its international economic position, and that it was required in order to make management roles more socially respected and more appealing to talented students. To fulfil this ambition, the UK government gave universities the task of equipping future managers with a broad education, delivered in a university-based business school context, thus bringing the standard of managers' knowledge and intellectual ability on a par with the knowledge and intellectual ability of graduates from other academic disciplines. Accomplishing this task of educating a new generation of highly knowledgeable and respected managers who would serve the needs of the British society and economy, on the other hand, called for a partnership between academia and industry, aimed at generating a positive impact on the country's economic development. Importantly, the success of this partnership relied on the understanding that both companies and universities had a responsibility for contributing to the nation's economic prosperity and international economic competitiveness. In other words, the expansion of UK higher education following the Robbins Report, including the creation of university-based management education, took place on the government's premise that rather than being independent of external interests and free to pursue knowledge for its own sake, universities had an important obligation to meet the society's needs, including the imperative to generate economic growth and wealth. As such, in the British academic context, the idea of universities' impact on society can be seen to have at least a six decades-long history. In the final section of this chapter, we discuss the multifaceted ways in which universities have and do impact society.

1.5 The multifaceted impact of universities

As our discussion so far has demonstrated, ideas about what universities' contribution to the society is and should be, have evolved over the recent centuries. Most significantly, ever since the early 1960s, in Britain, the notion that universities should contribute to the country's economic prosperity has influenced the government's policy towards HE, giving rise to the establishment and growth of business schools within universities. In parallel, after a long tradition of access to HE being restricted by social class (Mangan et al., 2010), universities were also given the task of driving social mobility through widening participation in higher education. Whilst HEIs engaged in WP work since the 1970s, these efforts have become particularly pronounced since 1997, following the publication of the Dearing Report – which addressed the issue of low participation in HE among individuals from disadvantaged socioeconomic backgrounds, as well as introducing tuition fees for university education – and the election of a Labour government. Widening participation, a project initially pursued by the 'polytechnic' and later 'post-1992 university' sector, over time became a concern for the entire HE sector in Britain, and was defined around the notion of 'fair access', i.e. 'access that is "equitable", that is, not denied on the basis of class, ethnicity, gender and so on' (McCaig, 2018: 53). In practice, post-1992 universities were understood to fulfil the mission of ensuring equality of access, whereas old, 'prestigious' universities were seen to enable equity, through non-discriminatory admissions processes, that would lead to upward social mobility for the most talented students from poor backgrounds. All these efforts have brought tangible societal outcomes. By contrast to the past when only a small fraction of the population entered HE, nearly 2.4 million students were registered to study at UK universities in 2018/19, which represented an increase by 74% compared to 1994. Over the quarter of a century between 1994 and 2019, the number of female university students increased by 133%, and during the 2010–2019 decade by 16%. In the same periods, the number of male students increased by 68% and 5%, respectively. Meanwhile, the volume of application acceptances rose by 50% for White students, 216% for Asian students, and 516% for Black students (Bolton, 2020).

Being agents of social mobility is not the only type of societal impact universities have. On the contrary, they interact with and influence the world around them in many ways, including but not limited to those defined through official impact measurement audits. As Addie (2017) suggests, universities affect local communities, cities, regions, and countries in at least seven distinct ways. First, universities themselves are 'economic engines'. They are places where innovation and entrepreneurship are generated, with a beneficial outcome for a range of industries. As major employers – in many cases, enjoying the status of the biggest and most desirable employer in a city or region – universities directly and indirectly support jobs at all levels of skills and qualifications. Further, they prepare students for employment through equipping them with knowledge, competences, and skills. Second, universities – through investment in buildings and campuses – change and shape the architectural landscape of the cities and regions in which they are based, and in doing this, also shape the local civic identities. Third, through recruiting international staff and students, they attract talent from across the world, who in turn contribute to economic prosperity. Fourth, both international staff and students play a vital cultural role in the local communities, enhancing their diversity and inclusivity. Their presence culturally and politically connects the UK to other countries, not least because both in the past and at present, many future political leaders have completed part or all of their HE in the UK (Coughlan, 2014). Fifth, academic research provides scientific evidence which forms the basis of public policy and as such, helps address societal challenges. For example, throughout the period of the COVID-19 pandemic, the UK government has repeatedly emphasised that its response to the coronavirus has been guided by 'scientific evidence' (www.gov.uk, 2020), whereas the government's Scientific Advisory Group for Emergencies (SAGE) has included academics employed by various British universities. In addition, universities' role in addressing societal challenges includes the provision of a range of services to local communities, from access to healthcare and sport facilities to opportunities for participation in cultural events such as theatre performances, arts exhibitions, and publicly available lectures. Sixth, universities play a crucial role in fostering creativity and stimulating open debate. The intellectual and artistic milieus that universities co-create contribute, on the one hand, to the country's global competitiveness through raising the status of a given city or region. On the other hand, universities are key sites where socially progressive ideas and movements flourish, and through this they shape the direction in which society and culture evolve. Seventh, according to Addie (2017), access to HE has a strong positive effect on lives, through enhancing self-knowledge and civic participation, as well as increasing people's employment opportunities.

1.6 Conclusion

The discussion presented in this chapter has focused on the evolution of the idea of universities' societal role. We have argued that whilst the understanding regarding what constitutes universities' impact has changed, for nearly 60 years now, universities in the UK have been explicitly expected to, and succeeded in, generating wide-ranging positive impact on society and economy. Our analysis has highlighted the tension between two contrasting views of universities and their societal role. One of these views, which we traced back to Humboldt's and Newman's 19th century thinking about universities, prioritises the pursuit of knowledge for knowledge's sake, and keeps in high regard universities' autonomy and independence of external influences. The other one, which in the UK context can be seen to have its roots in the post-WWII changes to the University Grant Committee's terms of reference, sees universities' main task in meeting national needs as defined by government policy, and places emphasis on the applied value of university knowledge and education. Whilst, according to the former view, there is no place for business and management education within a university context, the latter legitimises the presence of vocational subjects, such as management, as a necessary part of university education, seeing it as a vehicle for both economic development and social change through democratising and widening access to HE for students from disadvantaged backgrounds. The current model of university education in the UK reflects the latter view of universities' societal role. However, debates about the impact of universities and business schools carry within them echoes of Humboldtian and Newmanian ideas about universities and their broader relevance. In the next chapter, we further examine the contemporary understanding of the impact of universities, and business schools within them.

References

Addie, J.-P. (2017) Seven ways universities benefit society. *The Conversation*, 11th September, https://theconversation.com/seven-ways-universities-benefit-society-81072

Anderson, R., (2010) The idea of university today. *History and Policy.* http://www.historyandpolicy.org/policy-papers/papers/the-idea-of-a-university-today. Accessed 25 March 2021.

Bence, V. and Oppenheim, C. (2005) The evolution of the UK's Research Assessment Exercise: Publications, performance and perceptions. *Journal of Educational Administration and History*, 37 (2), 137–155.

Bolton, P. (2020) *Higher education student numbers.* Briefing paper no. 7857, 14th July. London: House of Commons Library.

Bourner, T. (2012) The history of UK business and management education. *Action Learning: Research and Practice*, 9 (1), 100–106.

Coughlan, S. (2014) One in seven countries has leader who studied in UK. https://www.bbc.co.uk/news/education-29361704. Accessed 25 March 2021.

Farrant, J. (1987) Central control of the university sector. *In*: T. Becher, ed. *British Higher Education.* London: Allen & Unwin.

Government Office for Science and Scientific Advisory Group for Emergencies (2020) Coronavirus (COVID-19): Scientific evidence supporting the UK government response. https://www.gov.uk/government/news/coronavirus-covid-19-scientific-evidence-supporting-the-uk-government-response. Accessed 25 March 2021.

Great Britain: Committee on Higher Education (1963) *Higher Education: Report of the Committee Appointed by the Prime Minister, under the Chairmanship of Lord Robbins, 1961–63.* Edited by Parliament of Great Britain. London: HMSO.

Kaelble, H. (1985) *Social mobility in the 19th and 20th centuries: Europe and America in comparative perspective.* Dover, NH: Berg.

Keeble, S.P. (1992) *The ability to manage: A study of British management, 1890–1990.* Manchester: Manchester University Press.

King, D. and Nash, V. (2001) Continuity of ideas and the politics of higher education expansion in Britain from Robbins to Dearing. *Twentieth Century British History*, 12 (2), 185–207.

Kipping, S.N. (1972) *Summing up*. London: Hutchinson.

Larson, M. (2020) Re-imagining management education in post-WWII Britain: views from government and business. *Management & Organization History*, 15 (2), 169–191.

Managing Training for Management (1963) *The Statist*. May 24, 563–564.

Mangan, J., Hughes, A., Davies, P. and Slack, K. (2010) Fair access: Locality, status and finance in students' choice of university. *Studies in Higher Education*, 35 (3), 335–350.

McCaig, C. (2018) English Higher Education: Widening participation and the historical context for system differentiation. *In*: M. Bowl, C. McCaig, and J. Hughes, eds. *Equality and differentiation in Higher Education*. London: Palgrave, 51–72.

McConnell, T., Berdahl, R. and Fay, M. (1973) *From elite to mass universal Higher Education: The British and American transformations*. Berkeley: University of California Press.

Nybom, T. (2003) The Humboldt legacy: Reflections on the past, present and future of the European university. *Higher Education Policy*, 16, 141–159.

Perkin, H. (2007) History of universities. *In*: J. Forest and P. Altbach, eds. *International handbook of Higher Education*. New York: Springer, 159–205.

Sanderson, M. (1972) *The universities and British industry, 1850–1970*. London: Routledge and Kegan Paul.

Tapper, E.R. and Salter, B.G. (1995) The changing idea of university autonomy. *Studies in Higher Education*, 20 (1), 59–71.

Vane, H. (1958) How will we manage? British industry suffers from unimaginative recruitment. *Crossbow*, 2, 32.

Wilson, J.F. and Thomson, A. (2006) *The making of modern management: British management in historical perspective*. Oxford: Oxford University Press.

2 Academic debates surrounding impact and relevance of BMS research

2.1 Introduction

For a number of years now, UK research councils have been instructed by government to link funded research to the requirements of industry users (Office of Science and Technology, 1993; Martin, 2011). Whilst much discussion of research impact has taken place in policymaking circles, such debate has also been conducted within academia. In tracing the genesis of academic discussions of research impact in the UK, Martin (2011) stresses work in the 1970s (Rip and Boeker, 1975; Nelkin, 1979) that highlighted the 'social responsibility of the scientist'. To quote Nelkin (1979: 181–182):

> Dependent on external funding, scientists often select their research less on the basis of scientific than on the organizational imperatives of their institutions. In this professional context, the notion of responsibility, and indeed of autonomy, assumes new dimensions. For as a resource, useful and utilized for policy purposes, science is subject to a host of political questions: Who has access to this resource? Is it equitably distributed? Who should control research and direct its priorities? And what are the appropriate institutions for control?

In the context of business and management studies (BMS), the importance of impact beyond academia has been vigorously contested through literature addressing the role of business schools in society (Burchell et al., 2015; Pettigrew and Starkey, 2016), and specifically through a body of work commonly referred to as the 'relevance debate' (Pettigrew, 1997; Hodgkinson and Starkey, 2011; Kieser et al., 2015; Irwin, 2019). Echoing Nelkin's (1979) view of science as a 'useful and utilized' resource that places a new responsibility on the scientist,

DOI: 10.4324/9781003090465-2

Pettigrew (1997: 347) – in the Special Issue of the *British Journal of Management* celebrating its 25th anniversary – suggested:

> It may be appropriate for some members of our local and international communities to raise their aspirations and deliver forms and processes of knowledge which meet the double hurdle of scholarly quality and policy/practice impact.

In this chapter, we discuss the key ideas found in research contributing to the relevance debate. We begin with introducing the 'relevance debate' in BMS literature, followed by an overview of the proposed solutions for increasing the relevance and impact of business schools' research. We then elaborate on the critical perspectives within the literature on relevance and impact on practice, before highlighting the need for extending our view of management practitioners to include business school students. In conclusion, we draw attention to the need to study organisational and individual consequences of the impact agenda.

2.2 The 'double hurdle' of rigour and relevance

The challenge to reconcile scholarly rigour with relevance to policy and practice has frequently been referred to as a 'double hurdle' (Pettigrew, 1997) faced by business and management studies scholars. Traditionally, research impact has been understood with reference to impact on the academic field, with citations typically considered as a proxy for research impact. This way of viewing impact, however, is not necessarily supportive of business schools' original mission to educate managers and to improve management practice. A focus on generating publications with a view to attract high citation counts incentivises academics to engage in 'scientification' (Butler et al., 2015; Carton and Mouricou, 2017) of their subject disciplines through becoming increasingly competent in the rigorous application of ever more sophisticated research methods, and through orienting their effort towards contributing to scholarly debates conducted with other academics. At the same time, prioritising scholarly quality in BMS research is considered unlikely to lead to outcomes that could easily gain practitioners' interest or even be comprehensible to a non-academic audience, contributing to the impression of management research being irrelevant, untranslatable, and unusable to management practice (Holmstrom et al., 2009). In this sense, the pursuit of scholarly rigour at the expense of engagement in practice can become potentially problematic for BMS as a field of research and for business schools as organisations. As Aguinis et al. (2014) observe, the preoccupation with citation levels as a vehicle for establishing institutional prestige and quality undermines the credibility of academic researchers outside the academic community. The potentially exclusionary consequences of this preoccupation have been widely acknowledged and even lamented in the management literature, as exemplified by Bennis and O'Toole's (2005: 103) article whose authors claim that: 'The dirty little secret at most of today's best business schools is that they chiefly serve the faculty's research interests and career goals, with too little regard for the needs of other stakeholders'.

On the other hand, it has also been recognised that 'the rigourous thinking and theoretical grounding that characterizes business school scholars and their research, actually offer an advantage over (…) the research that comes out of nonacademic sources' (Pfeffer and Fong, 2002: 93). However, in realising this advantage, and in overcoming the 'double hurdle' of rigour and relevance, BMS academics frequently encounter a 'double obstacle' of both not having and undervaluing the skills that are necessary to make research understandable, applicable, and credible to stakeholders outside academia (Tushman and O'Reilly III, 2007). As a result, a separation between what is considered high-quality management research and applied management practice continues to exist, as does the perception that BMS research is insufficiently relevant to practice, even though, it has been claimed that many academics actually have a preference for engagement in research projects with impact compared to those that only involve publications (Salter et al., 2017).

In the next sub-section, we discuss some of the suggestions found in the literature addressing the issue of how to make BMS research more relevant to practitioners, and how to reconcile the 'double hurdle' of rigour and relevance. Firstly, however, following Irwin (2019: 197), we would like to highlight the need to reflect on how terms such as 'rigour' and 'relevance' are 'defined, operationalized and understood in specific settings'. According to Irwin (2019), part of the difficulty with agreeing on whether and how rigour and relevance might be pursued simultaneously stems from the lack of agreement on what these terms mean. Irwin (2019) points out that both the quality of research and its societal value can be defined in a number of ways. He quotes the controversy around the *Academic Journal Guide* published by the Chartered Association of Business Schools in the UK, commonly referred to as the 'ABS Guide', as an example of how, within the field of business and management research, perspectives on how to determine the quality and value of research differ. The ABS list – a journal ranking list which is well-familiar to business school academics and deans not only in the UK but also internationally – has been described along a spectrum ranging from a 'recognised currency on which career progress can be based' (Association of Business Schools, 2015: 5), to having 'problematic unintended consequences' (British Academy of Management, 2015) and representing 'a symptom of a deeper malaise in business and management scholarship' (Tourish, 2015: 32). Following from this, as Irwin (2019: 203) argues, addressing the rigour-relevance gap is a complicated task not only because of the existence of the gap itself but also because of 'the role of "elite" journals in promoting certain interpretations of research excellence' and because of the contested views of what constitutes relevance, whereby it remains unclear if relevance denotes 'a "consultancy" approach, (...) dissemination and good communication, (...) or does it involve some form of engaged scholarship, critical evaluation or more challenging interaction with external stakeholders?' Based on his observations of the complexities surrounding the understandings of relevance, Irwin (2019) suggests a move away from framing academic work in terms of binary formulations, such as 'rigour' and 'relevance', and for 're-imagining' what we understand as quality of business school research. This ambitious but worthwhile project of 're-imagining' our understanding of quality of BMS research is yet to be fulfilled. At this stage, therefore, it is important to give an overview of existing contributions to discussions about how to make BMS research more impactful and relevant to practice.

2.3 Ideas for generating impactful and relevant BMS research

The issue of how to 'bridge the relevance gap' (Hodgkinson et al., 2001; Starkey and Madan, 2001) through conducting impactful business and management research has in itself become an important area of scholarly investigation by BMS scholars. Over the years, a range of solutions to the 'double hurdle' of rigour and relevance have been proposed.

For example, the seminal work by Tranfield and Starkey (1998) discusses the issue of rigour and relevance in the context of Gibbons et al.'s (1994) conceptualisation of 'mode 1' and 'mode 2' research. The former is characterised by a 'distinction between what is fundamental and what is applied; this implies an operational distinction between a theoretical core and other areas of knowledge such as the engineering sciences where the theoretical insights are translated into applications' (Gibbons et al., 1994: 19). Within this traditional academic model of knowledge production and dissemination, the research process is carried out by academics in elite universities, with little attention paid to the usability and application of this knowledge by practitioners. By contrast, in 'mode 2' research, there is a 'constant flow back and forth between the fundamental and the applied, between the theoretical and the practical. Typically, discovery occurs in contexts where knowledge is developed for, and put to, use, whilst results – which would have been traditionally characterised as applied – fuel further theoretical advances' (Gibbons et al., 1994: 19). Tranfield and Starkey (1998: 351) argue that mode 2 offers a 'potentially more appropriate (useful/ relevant) model of the link between theory and practice' and suggest its adoption for management research as an effective vehicle for overcoming the double hurdle of producing academic knowledge of high quality and being relevant to policy and practice. They see mode 2 research as requiring a transdisciplinarity and pluralist approach to generating knowledge.

In addition to mode 2 research, a number of other concepts and ideas have been put forward as part of the discussion about how to address the relevance gap, and it has been argued that separation of research from practice is harmful for both (Gulati, 2007). Hodgkinson and Starkey (2011, 2012), e.g. suggest that to bridge the relevance gap, researchers should, from the outset, design the process of producing and disseminating knowledge in a way that would make possible closer collaboration between academics and practitioners. Building on this, Marcos and Denyer (2012) explain how establishing such early stage collaboration facilitates the bringing together of theoretical and practical forms of knowledge in the research process. Adding to the debate, MacIntosh et al. (2012) argue for a move away from a simplistic view of academics as 'knowledge producers' and practitioners as 'knowledge consumers', in favour of a dialogical approach.

Moreover, expressions such as 'lost in translation' and 'lost before translation' have been introduced to signal, respectively, the issue of producing academic knowledge in a form that is incomprehensible to practitioners, and the problem of non-alignment between the interests and needs of academics and practitioners (Shapiro et al., 2007; Amara et al., 2019). Moreover, references to terms such as 'engaged scholarship' (Van de Ven and Johnson, 2006), 'triple helix of university-industry-government relations' (Etzkovitz and Leydesdorff, 2000), and 'evidence-based management' (Kieser et al., 2015), as well as calls for developing research in accordance with the principles of 'design science' and oriented towards 'practising the "we"' (Romme and Reymen, 2018; Kapasi and Rosli, 2020), all stress the importance of collaboration between academic researchers and research users bringing together 'their different perspectives and competencies to coproduce knowledge about a complex problem or phenomenon that exists under conditions of uncertainty found in the world' (Van de Ven and Johnson, 2006: 803) at different stages of knowledge production.

More recently, BMS scholars interested in impact have begun to pay closer attention to the complexities of academic–practitioner relationships (Bartunek and McKenzie, 2017) and to the importance of a longitudinal immersion in specific contexts (Wells and Nieuwenhuis, 2017) for generation of impactful research. For example, in a self-reflexive account of her long-term successful career as both a researcher and a management consultant, Empson (2017) considers her dual focus on producing academic research and engagement with practice in terms of a 'liminal life', one in which her involvement in consultancy work for a leading law firm has been akin to conducting an 'affair with the other' (Empson, 2013), and one which she wholeheartedly recommends to other academics. By contrast, Cunliffe and Scaratti (2017: 30) focus on the academic–practitioner relationship as a mode of engaged research that involves situated knowledge, dialogical sensemaking, and shared reflexivity, i.e.: 'creating a dialogue between conceptual and practical forms of expertise and knowledge (...), paying attention to people's contextualized work experiences; and developing an ability to create knowledge in uncertain and fluid situations that acknowledge the complexities of lived experience'. To Cunliffe and Scaratti (2017), collaborative conversations between academics and practitioners that take place during the research process can be vehicles for generating socially useful knowledge. Rather than focusing on the 'impact of', i.e. the outcomes of BMS research for organisations and society, the authors propose an 'impact-in' approach, showing how research can have impact – upon 'organizations, work, lives and selves immediately and in the longer term' (Cunliffe and Scaratti, 2017: 42) through its dialogical and reflexive process of co-generating knowledge.

In another example of an empirically rooted paper addressing the complexities of conducting impactful research, Sealy et al. (2017) conceptualise the process of impact generation through drawing on the concept of 'dialogic trading zones' (Romme and Reymen, 2018). They describe such trading zones as 'action-oriented encounters where the relationship between knowledge and practice is (...) co-constructed through evolving engagement with non-academic stakeholders' (Sealy et al., 2017: 65). The idea behind creating trading zones is to provide spaces where members of communities which operate according to different logics and motivations could come together, with a sense of shared purpose and responsibility for addressing problems (Romme and Reymen, 2018). Based on their own experience of conducting research in the area of Women on Boards, Sealy et al. (2017) discuss how impactful research, developed through practitioner–academic collaborations, is generated through a long-term engagement with a range of champions and diverse stakeholders in a given field, such as in the case of their own research, businesses, diversity experts, government policymakers, headhunters, key corporate individuals, media, and women themselves. They also highlight the 'indirect yet potent' (Sealy et al., 2017: 74) nature of the generated impact, demonstrating how, instead of the research impact being limited to a particular 'target audience', a range of parties have been affected by the research. Importantly, they draw attention to the dynamics of power and politics in trading zones, exemplified by potential tensions and disagreements that are likely to occur between different stakeholders, especially if, e.g. the research findings do not align with the expectations of government policymakers. In this context, they point to the importance of researchers' willingness to engage in politics and use political skill (Ferris et al., 2007), including 'social astuteness (recognizing evolving stakeholder agendas), interpersonal influence and networking ability (leveraging relationships to reconcile competing expectations)' (Sealy et al., 2017: 76). As Sealy et al.'s (2017) discussion demonstrates, the generation of impactful research through engagement with practitioners is a complex process, laden with politics and power, and presenting challenges to all parties involved. To provide further insights into the challenges and power-related aspects associated with producing impactful and relevant research, in the subsection below we focus on the critical perspectives articulates within the BMS impact debates.

2.4 Critical perspectives in debates around impact and relevance of BMS research

Notwithstanding various authors' recognition that it is necessary to move away from a situation in which much of academic research is produced and disseminated among a small group of peer researchers in a given discipline, with a shared understanding of specialist nomenclature (Cohen, 2007), the idea of academic–practitioner collaboration has also given rise to a range of researchers' concerns. Some authors, e.g. have questioned the often taken-for-granted assumption that the 'practitioner' is a manager, and in particular a senior manager. Instead, they have proposed the view of the practitioner as an activist (Willmott, 2008), 'the managed, (...) trade unionists, (...) women's groups and so on' (Fournier and Grey, 2000: 26), or the students (Anderson et al., 2017). In addition, a number of researchers have sought to critically interrogate and disrupt some of the 'common-sense' assumptions of the relevance debate, such as the taken-for-granted understanding of the pursuit of relevance as an inherently desirable and worthwhile objective of the business school (Knights, 2008; Nicolai and Seidl, 2010; Learmonth et al., 2012), and to examine the more problematic consequences, both for knowledge production and for academics who produce it, of the way in which impactful research is currently understood and pursued (Bresnen and Burrell, 2013; Empson, 2013; Butler et al., 2015). For instance, drawing on examples of research in finance and deconstruction, Learmonth et al. (2012) question the predominant characterisation of relevance as inherently 'good' and conceptually unproblematic, pointing to the entanglement of notions of usefulness and relevance with power and temporality. Their analysis draws attention to the relational nature of terms, such as 'relevance' and 'irrelevance', 'usefulness' and 'uselessness'. They highlight that what gets to be considered as useful and practically relevant research can be contingent upon the views of a small group of powerful actors, whose idea of usefulness is coloured by their own short-term interests, the pursuit of which has the potential to generate – as illustrated by the collapse of the sub-prime mortgage market and the subsequent Global Financial Crisis – disastrous consequences on a global scale. Based on their analysis, Learmonth et al. (2012) argue for reflexivity in relation to ideas about the usefulness and relevance of management research. In a similar vein, as a result of a critical reflection on issues of relevance of BMS research, Willmott (2012) suggests reframing relevance as 'social usefulness', whereas Sealy et al. (2017: 76) argue that 'relevance cannot be meaningfully discussed without considering the personal costs and trade-offs scholars face when engaging with external practitioners and organizations'.

Another set of insights into the relevance debate are offered by Carton and Mouricou (2017). Through a systematic literature review of journal articles addressing the rigour-relevance debate between 1994 and 2013, the authors identify four distinct, and often repeated, conceptions of relevance underpinning this body of work: 1) 'Gatekeepers' orthodoxy', relevant knowledge defined as 'knowledge that is spread to practitioners';

2) 'Collaboration with practitioners', relevant knowledge defined as 'knowledge that is useful to practitioners'; 3) 'Paradigmatic shift', relevant knowledge defined as 'knowledge that is interesting'; 4) 'Refocusing on common good', relevant knowledge defined as 'knowledge that makes sense and responds to the major issues facing the contemporary world' (Carton and Mouricou, 2017: 173). They conclude that over time, the latter two positions have been gaining in significance compared to the former two.

As far as empirical contributions to the critical perspectives on impact and relevance are concerned, Butler et al. (2015) explore the motivations, rewards, tensions, and ethical dilemmas that face leadership researchers when engaging with practitioners and taking on roles, such as management consultants, coaches, and providers of executive education. In contrast to the majority of scholars who have written about academic–practitioner engagement, Butler et al. (2015) draw attention to financial remuneration – and the implications of its existence – as one type of 'reward' which academics receive in exchange for engaging with organisational practitioners (see also Empson, 2017). The authors shed light on the conflicts which can arise between the pursuit of practitioner engagement and the accepted norms of scholarly conduct. They show how, through various compromises and trade-offs – including: modifying 'the norms of academic knowledge production to suit the demands of practitioners (...), limiting the scope of scholarly inquiry (...), lapsing into managerial cliché (...), [and] compromising [scholarly] identity (Butler et al., 2015: 738–739) – individual researchers seek to address these conflicts. Butler et al. (2015) also point to the varied, individually defined understandings of what 'positive impact' of research on practice means, coupled with a vagueness characterising attempts to describe in specific terms the extent to which scholars' engagement activities affect practitioners and organisations. Following from their study, the authors conclude that 'bringing academic research to bear on organizational issues (...) is not a straightforward process of knowledge transference, but a complex and fraught negotiation between differing norms and expectations, coloured by the rewards (material or otherwise) offered by organizations' (Butler et al., 2015: 740).

Using an auto-ethnographic lens, King and Learmonth (2015) discuss the complex practicalities and consequences of attempts to implement ideas developed within academia on management practice. Similar to Butler et al. (2015), they find that such attempts entail compromises and necessitate engagement in 'discomforting practices', going 'against the (...) ethos' (King and Learmonth, 2015: 361) of the intended initiative. Even though, according to Daniel King's theoretically informed personal narrative, there was a liberating dimension to his experience as a manager whose thinking was informed by critical scholarly ideas about management, in the end, his academic knowledge did not change his management practice but rather, motivated him to leave the world of management and to pursue an academic career. To us, a particularly interesting aspect of King's story is that he became a manager following and in parallel with studying management in a business school. In this sense, the dilemmas he faced in his management practice and the observations he made were interpreted by him through the lens of the knowledge he gained as a student. In the next sub-section, we focus on the so far under-developed aspect of understanding relevance and impact, namely the importance of recognising research impact that is produced through the educational process taking place in business schools.

2.5 The role of the educational process in generating impact on practice

As we have discussed above, notwithstanding continued contributions and developments, the literature about impact and relevance of BMS research is not without limitations. This is partly because, as Anderson et al. (2017) point out, the majority of discussions on how to address the 'double hurdle' of scholarly rigour and impact on practice focuses on the research project, in particular in the form of a journal article. Anderson et al. (2017: 14) critique the still widespread view that a 'highly starred and highly cited journal paper' is 'the most appropriate and important unit of analysis to measure the excellence of research and its impact'. They are also sceptical about the narrow understanding of management practitioners whom the impact debate typically defines as senior managers of organisations. Instead, drawing on a more pluralist view of impact (Aguinis et al. 2014), they bring attention to management education as the key activity carried out within business schools, and position all business school students – whom they see as either current or potential practitioners – as important stakeholders whose thinking and practice are impacted through the educational process. In proposing to view business school students at all levels as management practitioners, and thus moving away from the narrow view of practitioners as senior managers, Anderson et al. (2017: 19) see the possibility of diminishing 'the sense of separation and isolation' between management academics and practitioners. Relating to all students as practitioners would open up the space for management educators to evoke learners' sensitivities (Chia and Holt, 2008) and to inspire them. Within Anderson et al.'s (2017: 21) framework, business school academics make impact through 'relational management education interventions' that involve 'an engagement with theory as a means to inform practice and, vice versa, reflexive questioning and the consequent development of action strategies'.

Anderson et al.'s (2017) conceptualisation of impact has important implications not only for defining, but also for measuring research impact in business and management. The authors argue that with respect to impact, an academic's research work should not be assessed 'in isolation from the numerous other activities of academics: teaching, policy-work, consulting, institution-building and our academic administrative responsibilities' (Anderson et al., 2017: 17). Rather than referring to 'research impact', the authors suggest the use of 'researcher impact' or, preferably, 'academic impact', with the latter term recognising that the impact resulting from educational engagement of the academic with the students does not need to draw on the academic's own research. As we will discuss in the next chapter, the way in which impact measurement has been approached in the Research Excellence Framework is yet to embrace such a broader, and, following Anderson et al. (2017), more accurately reflective of the impacts made by BMS scholars on practice and policy outside academia, perspective on evaluating research impact.

2.6 Conclusion

In this chapter, we have addressed the academic debates concerning the relevance and impact of business and management research. Four key points emerge from our discussion. First, the debate continues, and efforts to (re-)conceptualise relevance and impact, propose solutions to the 'relevance gap', and highlight the problematic aspects of the impact and relevance agenda have, themselves, developed into a substantial body of BMS research. Second, whilst a lot of important insights have been gained through the development of this literature, only a small proportion of this work has involved an empirical study of producing impactful research, and – given the growing importance of impact evaluation as part of national governments' policy towards higher education – there is scope for further work illustrating the processes, challenges, and outcomes of engagement in impactful research. Third, the literature on impact and relevance of BMS research tends to privilege 'research' and 'research projects', with little attention paid to the individual and organisational aspects of impact generation, such as who produces impactful research and who does not; what engagement in research with impact on practice involves; and how engagement in this kind of research affect academics' careers as well as organisational inequalities and power relations. Fourth, the academic debates on impact and relevance of BMS research are underpinned by a narrow view of the 'management practitioner' which largely excludes business schools' students as current and future practitioners, and therefore also overlooks the importance of management education as a vehicle for generating impact by business school academics. In the next chapter, we continue with our discussion of BMS impact through a focus on the framing of impact within the UK's Research Excellence Framework, the policy framework for impact measurement adopted in in UK higher education.

References

Aguinis, H., et al. (2014) Scholarly impact: A pluralist conceptualization. *Academy of Management Learning and Education*, 13 (4), 623–639.

Amara, N., Olmos-Peñuela, J. and Fernández-de-Lucio, I. (2019) Overcoming the "lost before translation" problem: An exploratory study. *Research Policy*, 48 (1), 22–36.

Anderson, L., Ellwood, P. and Coleman, C. (2017) The impactful academic: Relational management education as an intervention for impact. *British Journal of Management*, 28 (1), 14–28.

Association of Business Schools. (2015) *Academic Journal Guide*. London, UK: Author.

Bartunek, J. and McKenzie, J., eds. (2017) *Academic-practitioner relationships: Developments, complexities and opportunities*. London: Routledge.

Bennis, W.G. and O'Toole, J. (2005, May) How business schools lost their way. *Harvard Business Review*, 83 (5), 96–104.

Bresnen, M. and Burrell, G. (2013) Journals a'la mode? Twenty years of living alongside Mode 2 and the new production of knowledge'. *Organization*, 20 (1), 25–37.

British Academy of Management. (2015, February 26) *The Association of Business Schools list of 'elite' journals* [Press release].

Burchell, J., Kennedy, S. and Murray, A. (2015) Responsible management education in UK business schools: Critically examining the role of the United Nations Principles for Responsible Management Education as a driver for change. *Management Learning*, 46 (4), 479–497.

Butler, N., Delaney, H. and Spoelstra, S. (2015) Problematizing "relevance" in the business school: The case of leadership studies. *British Journal of Management*, 26 (4), 731–744.

Carton, G. and Mouricou, P. (2017) Is management research relevant? A systematic analysis of the rigor-relevance debate in top-tier journals (1994–2013). *M@n@gement*, 20 (2), 166–203.

Chia, R. and Holt, R. (2008) The nature of knowledge in business schools. *Academy of Management Learning and Education*, 7 (4), 471–486.

Cohen, D.J. (2007) The very separate worlds of academic and practitioner publications in human resource management: Reasons for the divide and concrete solutions for bridging the gap. *Academy of Management Journal*, 50 (5), 1013–1019.

Cunliffe, A. and Scaratti, G. (2017) Embedding impact in engaged research: Developing socially useful knowledge through dialogical sensemaking. *British Journal of Management*, 28 (1), 29–44.

Empson, L. (2013) My affair with the "other": Identity journeys across the research-practice divide. *Journal of Management Inquiry*, 22 (2), 229–248.

Empson, L. (2017) My liminal life: Perpetual journeys across the research-practice divide. *In*: Bartunek, J. and McKenzie, J., eds. *Academic-practitioner relationships: Developments, complexities and opportunities*. London: Routledge.

Etzkovitz, H. and Leydesdorff, L. (2000) The dynamics of innovation: From National Systems and "Mode 2" to a Triple Helix of university-industry-government relations. *Research Policy*, 29 (2), 109–123.

Ferris, G.R., et al. (2007) Political skill in organizations. *Journal of Management*, 33 (3), 290–320.

Fournier, V. and Grey, C. (2000) At the critical moment: Conditions and prospects for critical management studies. *Human Relations*, 53 (1), 7–32.

Gibbons, M., Limoges, C., Nowotny, H., Schwartzman, S., Scott, P. and Trow, M. (1994) *The New Production of Knowledge: The Dynamics of Science and Research in Contemporary Societies*. London: Sage.

Gulati, R. (2007) Tent poles, tribalism, and boundary spanning: The rigor-relevance debate in management research. *Academy of Management Journal*, 50 (4), 755–782.

Hodgkinson, G.P. and Starkey, K. (2011) Not simply returning to the same answer over and over again: Reframing relevance. *British Journal of Management*, 22 (3), 355–369.

Hodgkinson, G.P. and Starkey, K. (2012) Extending the foundations and reach of design science: Further reflections on the role of critical realism. *British Journal of Management*, 23 (4), 605–610.

Hodgkinson, G.P., Herriot, P. and Anderson, N. (2001) Re-aligning the stakeholders in management research: Lessons from industrial, work and organizational psychology, *British Journal of Management*, 12 (s1), S41–S48.

Holmstrom, J., Ketokivi, M. and Hameri, A.-P. (2009) Bridging practice and theory: a design science approach. *Decision Sciences*, 40 (1), 65–87.

Irwin, A. (2019) Re-making 'quality' within the social sciences: The debate over rigour and relevance in the modern business school. *The Sociological Review*, 67 (1), 194–209.

Kapasi, I. and Rosli, A. (2020) The practice of "we": A framework for balancing rigour and relevance in entrepreneurship scholarship. *Journal of Business Venturing Insights*. 14 e00202, 1–8.

Kieser, A., Nicolai, A. and Seidl, D. (2015) The practical relevance of management research: Turning the debate on relevance into a rigorous scientific research program. *Academy of Management Annals*, 9 (1), 143–233.

King, D. and Learmonth, M. (2015) Can critical management studies ever be practical? A case study in engaged scholarship. *Human Relations*, 68 (3), 353–375.

Knights, D. (2008) Myopic rhetorics: Reflecting epistemologically and ethically on the demand for relevance in organizational and management research. *Academy of Management Learning and Education*, 7 (4), 537–552.

Learmonth, M., Lockett, A. and Dowd, K. (2012) Promoting scholarship that matters: The uselessness of useful research and the usefulness of useless research. *British Journal of Management*, 23 (1), 35–44.

MacIntosh, R., et al. (2012) Practising and knowing management: A dialogic perspective. *Management Learning*, 43 (4), 373–383.

Marcos, J. and Denyer, D. (2012) Crossing the sea from they to we? The unfolding of knowing and practising in collaborative research. *Management Learning*, 43 (4), 443–459.

Martin, B. (2011) The research excellence framework and the 'impact agenda': Are we creating a Frankenstein monster? *Research Evaluation*, 20 (3), 247–254.

Nelkin, D. (1979) The social responsibility of scientists. *Annals of the New York Academy of Sciences*, 334, 176–182.

Nicolai, A. and Seidl, D. (2010) That's relevant! Different forms of practical relevance in management science. *Organization Studies*, 31 (9–10), 1257–1285.

Office of Science and Technology. (1993) Realising our potential: A strategy for Science, Engineering and Technology. *Cmnd. 2250*. London: HMSO.

Pettigrew, A.M. (1997) The double hurdles for management research. *In*: T. Clarke, ed. *Advancement in Organizational Behaviour: Essays in honour of Derek S. Pugh*. London: Dartmouth Press, 277–296.

Pettigrew, A.M. and Starkey, K. (2016) From the Guest Editors: The legitimacy and impact of business schools – Key issues and a research agenda. *Academy of Management Learning and Education*, 15 (4), 649–664.

Pfeffer, J. and Fong, C.T. (2002) The end of business schools? Less success than meets the eye. *Academy of Management Learning and Education*, 1, 78–95.

Rip, A. and Boeker, E. (1975) Scientists and social responsibility in the Netherlands. *Social Studies of Science*, 5 (4), 457–484.

Romme, A. and Reymen, I. (2018) Entrepreneurship at the interface of design and science: Toward an inclusive framework. *Journal of Business Venturing Insights*, 10 e00094, 1–8.

Salter, A., Salandra, R. and Walker, J. (2017) Exploring preferences for impact versus publications among UK business and management academics. *Research Policy*, 46 (10), 1769–1782.

Sealy, R. et al. (2017) Expanding the notion of dialogic trading zones for impactful research: The case of Women on Boards research. *British Journal of Management*, 28 (1), 64–83.

Shapiro, D.L., Kirkman, B.L. and Courtney, H.G. (2007) Perceived causes and solutions of the translation problem in management research. *Academy of Management Journal* 50 (2), 249–266.

Starkey, K. and Madan, P. (2001) Bridging the relevance gaps: aligning stakeholders in the future of management research. *British Journal of Management*, 12 (Special Issue), S3–S26.

Tourish, D. (2015) March 19. Rank irrelevance. *Times Higher Education*, p. 32.

Tranfield, D. and Starkey, K. (1998) The nature, social organization and promotion of management research: towards policy. *British Journal of Management*, 9 (4), 341–353.

Tushman, M.L. and C. O'Reilly III. (2007) Research and relevance: Implications of Pasteur's quadrant for doctoral pro- grams and faculty development. *Academy of Management Journal*, 50, 769–774.

Van de Ven, A.H. and Johnson, P.E. (2006) Knowledge for theory and practice. *Academy of Management Review*, 31, 902–921.

Wells, P. and Nieuwenhuis, P. (2017) Operationalizing deep structural sustainability in business: Longitudinal immersion as extensive engaged scholarship. *British Journal of Management*, 28 (1), 45–63.

Willmott, H. (2008) Critical management and global justice. *Organization*, 15 (6), 927–931.

Willmott, H. (2012) Reframing relevance as 'social usefulness': A comment on Hodgkinson and Starkey's 'Not simply returning to the same answer over and over again'. *British Journal of Management*, 23 (4), 598–604.

3 Framing impact

3.1 Introduction

In the previous two chapters, we first traced the historical development of thinking about universities' societal role, pointing to the gradual increase in the nation states' involvement in determining and assessing the economic and social usefulness of higher education institutions; subsequently, we elaborated on the academic debates on relevance and impact of business and management research. In this chapter, we focus on the UK government's policy framework for evaluating the quality of research conducted by higher education institutions, i.e. the Research Excellence Framework, and discuss how research impact is framed by the UK policymakers.

On the one hand, the demand for universities' accountability in terms of the use of resources may seem an obvious and non-controversial requirement. Universities, after all, have an important function to fulfil and since they operate under conditions of resource constraints, ensuring that their activities benefit the nation should not be surprising. There is, however, a 'dark side' to the idea that universities' activities need to be subject to close external scrutiny, as if without this scrutiny, the societal usefulness and legitimacy of universities were in doubt. Arguably, explicitly expressing doubt in the value of the work carried out within universities can be seen as an aspect of the spread of anti-intellectual populist political discourse (White, 1962; Bourdieu, 2016) across the world. Therefore, in this chapter, we first locate the current emphasis on ensuring the accountability of universities, especially in the UK, against the broader *Zeitgeist* of anti-intellectualism and populism (see Kerr and Śliwa, 2020). Further, we explore the specific definition of impact as articulated within the UK's Research Excellence Frameworks (REF2014 and REF2021). We point out that this definition and the underlying

DOI: 10.4324/9781003090465-3

understanding of the impact of research have been developed from within the science disciplines. Through an examination of the composition of the template used for the purpose of impact submissions, we explain why the current way of defining and measuring impact might not be adequately capturing some of the aspects of impact generated by business schools. In conclusion, we highlight the need to understand the generation of impact in terms of the organisational processes and practices that have consequences for organisational inequalities, hierarchies, and power relations, as well as the careers of individual academics.

3.2 Populist politics and the *Zeitgeist* of resentment and distrust of expertise

One of the most controversial statements of the UK's Brexit referendum campaign was the interview contention of Michael Gove, at the time, the UK Justice Secretary, that 'people in this country have had enough of experts' (Mance, 2016). This declaration captured for many the growing distrust in a section of the electorate of experts, which we might classify, loosely speaking, as academics, economic forecasters, and scientists. More generally, this distrust – a long-recognised characteristic of populist anti-intellectualism (White, 1962) – helped mobilise the growth of populism internationally (Rodrik, 2018), through a simple message constructed to appeal to the so-called left-behind voters (Crutzen et al., 2020), and aimed at convincing them to cast their vote in favour of Brexit.

The concept of populism itself has been defined with reference to 'a rhetoric claiming that the only legitimate authority flows directly from "the people", and by contrast "the establishment" is corrupt, out of touch and self-serving, betraying the public trust, and thwarting the popular will' (Norris, 2020: 2). Moreover, Norris stresses that whilst previous studies have typically identified populist rhetoric as emanating from the radical or extreme right, a less tightly bounded set should include parties considered either left-wing or progressive. Prior work, therefore – one might conclude – may have even underestimated the extent of populism. In putting forward a Bourdieu-inspired framework for analysing Brexit in the context of populist politics, Kerr and Śliwa (2020: 499) suggest an understanding of populism as 'a political methodology operationalised by demagogues to mobilise forms of *ressentiment*'. Kerr and Śliwa (2020: 496) describe *ressentiment* as a 'feeling of powerlessness that permeates certain social groups (…) who feel that they are being unjustly denied their rightful position of socio-cultural dominance due to a perceived dual cultural threat from alien "others" and the machinations of unaccountable "elites"'. In this context, Gove's (2016) statement that the 'people (...) have had enough of experts' can be seen as an articulation and reinforcement of *ressentiment* towards the 'elites', and specifically towards the educated sections of the British society, represented, e.g. by academics engaging in scholarly research. Kerr and Śliwa (2020: 496) argue that the Leave campaign strategists used the populist rhetoric to gain support from two societal fractions:

(1) members of the traditional working class who feel themselves economically deprived and 'left behind' (see, e.g. Pettifor, 2017) by de-industrialisation and financialisation (ascribed to globalisation as promoted by economic elites) and (2) the relatively economically privileged who feel that (what they perceive as) their 'native, white' social and cultural dominance (Golec de Zavala et al., 2017) has been threatened by 'multiculturalism' in the form of an influx of people speaking different languages, eating different foods, and following different religions.

Meanwhile, the growth in numbers of the left-behind, or those who believe themselves marginalised by mainstream parties, is clearly linked to the growth in inequality in several OECD countries in the latter half of the 20th and early part of the 21st century (Makhlouf et al., 2021). Crutzen et al. (2020: 2) note that populist politicians, in appealing to the marginalised, emphasise the common-sense wisdom of the people over the specialised knowledge of experts and that accordingly 'tend to ignore expert advice, resulting in, for example, climate change scepticism or policies that disregard basic economic reasoning'. Such thinking is perhaps reinforced by the ability for geographically disparate political groups to connect via the internet (Colleoni et al., 2014) as illustrated, e.g. by the Google Trends search volume index (SVI) of 'Climate change hoax.'

SVI represents the relative proportion of a search string relative to all strings and then indexed from 1 to 100, running from least to most popular. Here, Figure 3.1 clearly shows that 'Climate change hoax' has been a popular search on Google over the recent past, suggesting that large numbers of people shape their views on globally significant issues, such as the climate change using sources other than scientific proof. Similarly, distrust of experts can be evidenced by the significant proportion of the population unwilling to participate in the COVID immunisation programme. According to a survey conducted in the

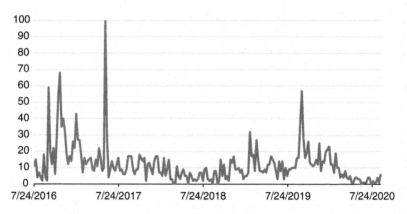

Figure 3.1 Worldwide Google Trends Search Volume Index (SVI) 'Climate change hoax'.

Source: Google Trends https://trends.google.co.uk/trends/explore?date=today%205-y& q=Climate%20change%20hoax

UK at the end of November 2020, only 42% of the respondents confirmed that they would 'definitely' take a COVID-19 vaccine, whereas a large proportion admitted to being cautious towards or outright against the vaccine, despite the repeated messaging from academic experts and the government that 'the science is clear – vaccines save lives' (Wallis, 2020).

Within this *Zeitgeist* of expert distrust and resentment, the UK became the first country to undertake a formal assessment of its universities' impact outside the immediate academic sphere. This occurred within REF 2014 and alongside evaluations of academic outputs and research environment, which had been carried out in previous exercises. Whilst 'value for money' assessments have been common in public sector accounting, the idea of universities as an independent authority and consequently, arbiters of their own activities as explored in Chapter 1, arguably protected higher education institutions (HEIs) from such investigations (see also Irvine and Martin, 1984). The extent of the erosion of this view in the UK is perhaps most profoundly indicated by the inclusion of impact measurement in REF 2014, asserting that academics need to prove their 'use value' to the government. One might even go further and suggest that the underlying assumption here seems to be that academics cannot be trusted to be useful to society, and therefore their value has to be closely monitored and measured. In this manner, they have to legitimise their presence, and – given a particular definition of impactful behaviour – universities' activities can be directed in a desired fashion.

Of course, once one has decided to assess impact of universities, decisions are required over the dimension(s) of impact and type of measurement. Arguably, as we have discussed in Chapter 1, universities have multidimensional impacts including research, education, cultural, consultancy, and broad economic impacts that could be formally assessed. For example, a report by Oxford Economics (2017) noted that UK Universities generated a gross output of £95 billion in 2014–2015, accounted for approximately 2.9% of GDP and supported 940,000 jobs. Moreover, Welsh universities produced output of more than £5 billion in 2015–2016 and underpinned approximately 50,000 jobs (Viewforth Consulting, 2018) whilst Valero and Van Reenen (2019) in a global analysis showed that universities are associated with higher economic growth and positive spillover effects into local areas. The sector is clearly vital to the UK economy but by assessing the impact of research rather than other dimensions, the REF exercise challenges the notion of academics as experts with inherent value and authority. Additionally, whilst the measurement of economic impacts has a more established base, the measurement of research impact is relatively nascent and still heavily contestable. Therefore, it is important to examine in more detail the REF template for evaluating impact in REF2014 and REF2021. This is where we turn next.

3.3 The UK's Research Excellence Framework 2014 (REF 2014)

Traditionally, the idea of research impact was understood with reference to academic impact which implies 'research, which breaks the dominant paradigm and influences future research investigations' (Reale et al., 2018: 299). A range of bibliometric methods have been developed to measure the intellectual contribution to a particular academic field of study (Wolf et al., 2013) through proxies such as the number of citations, the quantity and rank of publications, and/or h-index which measures both the productivity and citation impact of an author's publications. By contrast to these well-established measures of individual scholars' or publications' academic impact, REF 2014 was the first countrywide evaluation of university activity that assessed the impact of the research outside the academic sector. Specifically, impact was defined as:

> For the purposes of the REF, impact is defined as an effect on, change or benefit to the economy, society, culture, public policy or

services, health, the environment or quality of life, beyond academia (REF 02.2011: 26).

As Kellard and Śliwa (2016) note, the phrasing 'effect on, change or benefit', does not make it explicitly clear whether it matters if the impact is adjudged positive or negative. The guidance subsequently partially addresses this issue by stating: 'Impact includes the reduction or prevention of harm, risk, cost or other negative effects' (REF 02.2011: 26). To enable the evaluation of research impact, participating Units of Assessment (UoAs) were expected to submit a set of impact case studies, accompanied by an impact template. The number of individual impact case studies submitted by each UoA was computed relative to the number of staff submitted. Specifically, units submitting up to 14.99 FTE staff members were required to produce two impact case studies, with an additional case study required for each interval of 10 FTE staff submitted. The case studies were given a weighting of 80%, with the impact template contributing 20%. When assessing the impact case studies submitted by institutions, panels were instructed to evaluate 'reach and significance', with reach described as: 'the spread or breadth of influence or effect on the relevant constituencies' (REF 01.2012: 34) and significance: 'the intensity of the influence or effect' (ibid).

REF 2014 panels assessed the criteria jointly and gave impact scores between four stars, considered 'outstanding', and one star, categorised as 'recognised but modest'. The remaining case studies were evaluated as 'unclassified' meaning either presenting 'little or no reach and significance', 'not eligible' or 'not underpinned by excellent research produced by the submitted unit' (REF 02.2011: 44). On this latter point, 'excellent research' was categorised as research outputs evaluated as at least 'two star'; i.e. 'quality that is recognised internationally in terms of originality, significance and rigour' (REF 02.2011: 29). Moreover, this underpinning research needed to have been generated within the submitting HEI over the 21-year interval between 1 January 1993 and 31 December 2013; this can be contrasted with the locus of impact, which was a shorter five and a half year period between 1 January 2008 and 31 July 2013.

HEIs were advised that they should present their 'strongest examples of impact that are underpinned by the submitted unit's excellent research' (REF 02.2011: 28), whereby such strength was to be illustrated in a case study pro-forma which, amongst other things, provided details of the underpinning research, the impact, and evidence that corroborated the impact. The type of evidence could include, e.g. 'reports in the public domain, confidential reports, web links and testimonials from users or individual beneficiaries' (REF 02.2011: 56). Moreover, the evidence needed to clearly demonstrate a 'strong enabling connection between the listed research and the impact described' (REF 02.2011: 29).

3.4 Second time around: REF 2021

Conducting REF evaluations is a time- and resource-consuming process. Whilst the deadline for submissions to REF 2014 was 29 November 2013, the results of the assessment were announced just over a year later, on 18 December 2014. Because of the resource-intensity of the exercise, the conclusion of each REF cycle raises questions about whether further REF exercises would be conducted in the future. Following REF 2014, a decision was made that a subsequent REF would be taking place, with an initial deadline of 27 November 2020, postponed to 31 March 2021 as a result of the COVID-19 pandemic. This means that the considered time period for impact was extended to cover the period between 1 August 2013 and 31 December 2020 (REF 02.2020) – a larger seven and a half year interval, although the allowed period for the underpinning research remained the same as originally announced, at 1 January 2000 to 31 December 2020.

At least from a HEFCE point of view, REF2014 and in particular, the introduction of the impact component was considered relatively successful (see Manville et al., 2015). To further strengthen the importance of the assessment of research impact outside academia as an indicator of a university's value in the eyes of the policymaker and as a criterion behind the distribution of public funding among HEIs, the weighting of impact in REF2021 has been increased to 25% from 20% in 2014 (REF 01.2019: 7). Otherwise, the broad contours of impact exercises in REF2014 and REF2021 have remained analogous; e.g. the definition of impact along with the assessment criteria of reach and significance have stayed the same. However, the sphere of where impact can occur for REF purposes has been slightly but, at least potentially, significantly altered. In particular, for REF 2014, HEFCE guidance suggests that 'Impacts on students, teaching or other activities within the submitting HEI are *excluded*' (REF 02.2011: 48; emphasis added); whereas in REF 2021, 'Impacts on students, teaching or other activities both within and/or beyond the submitting HEI are *included*'. (REF 01.2019:68). This extension of spheres in which research impact can be evidenced over impacts on students has allowed impact types, such as 'reduced gap in academic achievement for students with protected characteristics' or 'influencing the design and delivery of curriculum' (REF 02.2019: Annex A) to be newly included when the impact is within the institution. This addition of the impacts on students can be seen as an attempt on HEFCE's part to demonstrate sensitivity towards the ways in which universities, through their research, address issues of equality, diversity, and inclusion among students.

3.5 Problematising the current framing of impact in the REF

In their analysis of the REF 2014 impact submissions to the Business and Management Unit of Assessment, Kellard and Śliwa (2016) discuss, among other things, the potentially distortionary effect of the framing of impact in the REF2014 exercise. 'Framing' in this context relates to the particular definition and measurement criteria of impact, which, arguably, are not appropriately rendered to cover all the relevant types of impact produced by business and management scholars (see Willmott, 2012). This is important, especially given the recognition in the literature that impact evaluation can be easier in certain disciplines than others (Williams and Grant, 2018). In this context, the UK REF 2014 and REF 2021 approach appears problematic, as it requires institutions to demonstrate, in a convincing and unambiguous manner, a causal link between underpinning research and specific outcomes. For example, Penfield et al. (2014: 6) comment:

> This presents particular difficulties in research disciplines conducting basic research, such as pure mathematics, where the impact of research is unlikely to be foreseen. Research findings will be taken up in other branches of research and developed further before socio-economic impact occurs, by which point, attribution becomes a huge challenge. If this research is to be assessed alongside more applied research, it is important that we are able to at least determine the contribution of basic research.

The design of impact assessment in UK REF is heavily influenced by the Australian Research Quality Framework (RQF). Although only recently operationalised in an impact context (see Australian Research Council, 2018), the RQF was the first example of an all-disciplines exercise to assess the explicit impact of research itself and posited many of the features we currently observe in the UK impact assessment framework, including using narrative case studies as the vehicle for making and evidencing impact claims (Penfield et al., 2014). Prior models tended to be employed in the health sciences (Grant, 2006); in this vein, the Payback Framework (Nason et al., 2008; Hanney and González-Block, 2011) contains academic research and associated socio-economic outcomes to substantiate past research funding and buttress applications for future awards (Penfield et al., 2014). It is possible that such models may allow for adequately capturing impact in some sciences. For example, the development of an effective vaccine for COVID-19 can be tied directly to clear health, social, and economic benefits. However, as Kellard and Śliwa (2016) point out, in the social sciences per se, and business and management studies specifically, the construction and assertion of academic knowledge often takes place via debate in the literature between otherwise independent researchers, and attribution to a single or small group of scholars of a specific impact outcome is either difficult to trace or quite simply, leads to disingenuous results (Smith et al., 2011; Sivertsen and Meijer, 2020). This 'attribution problem' is non-trivial and as noted above, similarly obtains when there is a significant time lag between the research taking place and impact occurring. Further, efforts to evaluate the societal impact of social sciences research also encounter the 'causality problem', whereby it is often unclear which impact can be attributed to which cause in terms of research and innovation activities, inputs, and outputs, as well as the 'evaluation timescale problem' and the associated risk of emphasis on short-term benefits (Lindgreen et al., 2020). To illustrate the issue with 'evaluation timescale', Learmonth et al. (2012) give the example of the Cambridge mathematician, G.H. Hardy, whose work on pure mathematics was – to the scholar's great regret (Hardy, 1940) – 'practically irrelevant' during his professional career, but later on became of key use in the development of modern computing.

It is important to note that the design of the impact evaluation framework in both REF 2014 and REF 2021 does contain elements to allow a generic discipline approach. Whilst earlier models often contained data driven evaluation tools such as financial return, bibliometrics, or benchmarking (Grant, 2006), the primacy of the case study within REF allows the included narratives to be discipline-specific, presenting qualitative information effectively and addressing particular stakeholder groups in a manner that would not be possible (Penfield et al., 2014) if one were to employ a more numbers-based evaluation methodology. In this latter work, Penfield et al. (2014) also list some drawbacks of the case study approach including that the very subject specificity of the method makes comparisons of impact between disciplines problematic. To this end, the authors pose a pertinent question: 'Case studies are ideal for showcasing impact, but should they be used to critically evaluate impact?' (Penfield et al., 2014: 9). However, in an attempt to circumvent such criticism, the criteria of 'reach' and 'significance' are employed alongside the case study approach in order to facilitate intra-disciplinary comparisons (see Scoble et al., 2010). Interestingly, for the impact exercise in REF 2014, the Business and Management unit of assessment scored less highly than many of the 'sciences' (Kellard and Śliwa, 2016).

Despite the centrality of 'reach' and 'significance', the REF impact framework underplays and therefore, arguably, undermines the notion that scholars' most important impacts, including the impacts of their research, will occur through teaching (see also Anderson et al., 2017). This seems particularly anomalous in the case of business schools, given – as discussed in Chapter 1 – the rationale for their establishment rested on the premise of educating managers and disseminating excellent management practice (see also Starkey and Tiratsoo, 2007). Indeed, and as stated earlier in this chapter, whilst REF 2014 guidelines allowed for research impact to occur within the educational sphere, 'Impacts on students, teaching or other activities within the submitting HEI [were] excluded'. As a consequence, this resulted in very few educationally focused case studies being submitted to the UK exercise.

Compared to impact assessment in REF2014, the REF2021 guidance did indicate some positive changes to the remit for impact activities, allowing educational impacts 'both within and/or beyond the submitting HEI' (REF 01.2019: 68). However, it is instructive that in the many examples of impacts and indicators (see REF 02.2019: Annex A) 'Impacts on understanding, learning and participation' are listed last of several areas of impact and therefore behind 'Impacts on the health and wellbeing of people, and animal welfare', 'Impacts on social welfare', 'Impacts on creativity, culture and society', 'Impacts on commerce and the economy', and 'Impacts on public policy, law and services', to mention a few. Thus, whilst the REF 2021 framework acknowledges that an HEI's own students are a constituency, it does not seemingly open up the possibility of acknowledging business schools' teaching activity as (i) the key activity business school academics engage in and (ii) an activity that requires a high level of knowledge that needs to be updated on a regular basis, i.e. through a person's involvement in research. In blunt terms, the largest impact in which business schools are engaged is typically ignored. This neglect of impact through teaching can be considered to be based on the misguided assumption that because demonstrating a direct link between, on the one hand, the content and the outcomes of the students' education and, on the other, the research produced by academic staff in the business school in which the students were educated is not easy and straightforward, the multi-faceted outcomes of this education on students are considered as unconnected to the research produced by the business school's staff.

Indeed, educational impact is not the only area which is likely underestimated by the current REF. As Kellard and Śliwa (2016: 709) argue, given that the underpinning research for impact case studies had to present at least a two-star ranking, many non-research intensive business schools found it challenging to 'showcase their long established engagement with industry and their influence on management and organizational practice through the work of those staff who are active in applied research and knowledge transfer activity'. Taken as a whole, it appears that, despite changes in impact assessment guidance that have taken place between REF 2014 and REF 2021, the REF exercise continues to be very narrow in scope, capturing only a small fraction of the variety and import of impact that business schools provide in the UK.

3.6 Conclusion

This chapter has addressed the framing of impact within the UK's current research excellence framework. We began by highlighting the wider context in which such evaluations have developed; in particular, we have noted how the populist political discourse, manifested, e.g. through pro-Brexit rhetoric, has served to undermine both the political and public standing of academics as autonomous experts. We then emphasised two key notions as underlying the current framing of impact in the REF. The first underscores the direct 'causal link' that the REF guidelines require institutions to demonstrate between the underpinning research and specific impact outcomes. This gives rise to the 'attribution problem' in disciplines such as social sciences, where research knowledge is often constructed among many independent scholars over time. In addition, and with particular relevance to the impact generated by business schools, it also disregards many academics in UK business schools who, whilst considered to be 'non-research active' in REF terms, nevertheless apply their subject knowledge to generate significant impacts within local, national, and international contexts.

The second notion emphasises that some areas of impact are privileged over others in the REF guidance. In particular, it is noticeable that educational impacts are much less visible, resulting in very few educationally focused case studies submitted to REF 2014 by business and management Units of Assessments. The overlooking of such a key area produces a skewed and very partial view of the impacts that business schools in the UK provide.

The inclusion of impact within the REF also has implications for the organisational processes and practices that academics work within and carry out. Preparing impact submissions constitutes a burdensome process for universities, it is not always easily reconciled with other aspect of work, and certain groups of academics, including women and early career researchers, are routinely excluded from the networks that facilitate and produce impact. In the next chapter, we discuss in more detail a range of consequences for different groups of academics, and for organisational inequalities, hierarchies, and power relations, of the way in which the generation of impact is currently approached within the research excellence framework.

References

Anderson, L., Ellwood, P. and Coleman, C. (2017) The impactful academic: Relational management education as an intervention for impact. *British Journal of Management*, 28 (1), 14–28.

Australian Research Council. (2018) *EI 2018 Assessment Handbook*. Canberra: Commonwealth of Australia.

Bourdieu, P. (2016) *Sociologie Generale Vol 2: Cours au Collège de France 1983–1986*. Paris: Seuil.

Colleoni, E., Rozza, A. and Arvidsson, A. (2014) Echo chamber or public sphere? Predicting political orientation and measuring political homophily on Twitter using big data. *Journal of Communication*, 64 (2), 317–332.

Crutzen, B., Sisak, D. and Swank, O. (2020) Left behind voters, anti-elitism and popular will. Tinbergen Institute Discussion Paper, TI 2020-055/VII.

Golec de Zavala, A., Guerra, R. and Simão, C. (2017) The relationship between the Brexit vote and individual predictors of prejudice: Collective narcissism, right wing authoritarianism, social dominance orientation. *Frontiers in Psychology*, 8, 1–14.

Grant, J. (2006) Measuring the benefits from research. *RAND Europe*. http://www.rand.org/pubs/research_briefs/2007/RAND_RB9202.pdf. Accessed 18 December 2020.

Hanney, S. and González-Block, M.A. (2011) Yes, research can inform health policy; but can we bridge the 'do-knowing it's been done' gap? *Health Research Policy and Systems*, 9, 23.

Hardy, G.H. (1940) *A mathematician's apology*. Cambridge: Cambridge University Press.

Irvine, J. and Martin, B.R. (1984) What direction for basic scientific research? In: M. Gibbons, P. Gummett and B. Udgaonkar, eds. *Science and Technology Policy in the 1990s and Beyond*. Harlow: Longman, 67–98.

Kellard, N.M. and Śliwa, M. (2016) Business and management impact assessment in REF2014: Analysis and reflection. *British Journal of Management*, 27 (4), 693–711.

Kerr, R. and Śliwa, M. (2020) When the political becomes (painfully) personal: Org-studying the consequences of Brexit. *Organization*, 27 (3), 494–505.

Learmonth, M. , Lockett, A. and Dowd, K. (2012) Promoting scholarship that matters: the uselessness of useful research and the usefulness of useless research. *British Journal of Management*, 23 (1), 35–44.

Lindgreen. A., et al. (2021) Editorial: How to define, identify and measure societal value. *Industrial Marketing Management*, 97, A1–A13.

Makhlouf, Y., Kellard, N. and Vinogradov, D. (2021) Income inequality and social values: A long-term relationship. Working Paper.

Mance, H. (2016) 'Britain has had enough of experts', says Gove. *Financial Times*, 3 June.

Manville, C., et al. (2015) Preparing impact submissions for REF 2011: An evaluation (Findings and observations). *Rand Europe*. HEFCE.

Nason, E., et al. (2008) Health research – Making an impact. The economic and social benefits of HRB-funded research. *Rand Europe*. Dublin: Health Research Board.

Norris, P. (2020) Measuring populism worldwide. Harvard Kennedy School Faculty Research Working Paper, RWP20-002.

Oxford Economics (2017) The Economic Impact of Universities in 2014–15: Report for Universities UK.

Penfield, T., Scoble, R. and Wykes, M.C. (2014) Assessment, evaluations, and definitions of research impact: A review. *Research Evaluation*, 23 (1), 21–32.

Pettifor, A. (2017) Brexit and its consequences. *Globalizations*, 14 (1), 127–132.

Reale, E., et al. (2018) A review of literature on evaluating the scientific, social and political impact of social sciences and humanities research. *Research Evaluation*, 27(4), 298–308.

Rodrik, D. (2018) Populism and the economics of globalization. *Journal of International Business Policy*, 1 (1–2), 12–33.

Scoble, R., et al. (2010) Institutional strategies for capturing socio-economic impact of academic research. *Journal of Higher Education Policy and Management*, 32 (5), 499–510.

Siversten, G. and Meijer, I. (2020) Normal versus extraordinary societal impact: How to understand, evaluate and improve research activities in their relations to society? *Research Eveluation*, 29 (1), 211–218.

Smith, S., Ward, V., and House, A. (2011) "Impact" in the proposals for the UK's Research Excellence Framework: Shifting the boundaries of academic autonomy. *Research Policy*, 40 (10), 1369–1379.

Starkey, K. and Tiratsoo, N. (2007) *The business school and the bottom line.* Cambridge: Cambridge University Press.

Valero, A. and Van Reenen, J. (2019) The economic impact of universities: Evidence from across the globe. *Economics of Education Review*, 68 (C), 53–67.

Viewforth Consulting (2018) The economic impact of Higher Education in Wales: Report to Universities Wales. Viewport Consulting and Universities Wales, http://www.uniswales.ac.uk/media/UNI010-Economic-Impact-Report_ FINAL.pdf. Accessed on 22 September 2021.

Wallis, W. (2020) How anti-vaxxers are threatening the UK's Covid programme. *Financial Times*, 30th November.

White, M. (1962) Reflections on anti-intellectualism. *Daedalus*, 91, 457–468.

Williams, K. and Grant, J. (2018) A comparative review of how the policy and procedures to assess research impact evolved in Australia and the UK. *Research Evaluation*, 27 (2), 93–105.

Willmott, H. (2012) Reframing relevance as "social usefulness": A comment on Hodgkinson and Starkey's "Not simply returning to the same answer over and over again". *British Journal of Management*, 23 (4), 598–604.

Wolf, B., et al. (2013) Evaluating research beyond scientific impact: How to include criteria for productive interactions and impact on practice and society. *GAIA – Ecological Perspectives on Science and Society*, 22 (2), 104–114.

4 The influence of the impact agenda on organisational inequalities

4.1 Introduction

In the previous chapter, we discussed the principles underlying the Research Excellence Framework (REF) in the UK, with a special emphasis on rules guiding the assessment of research impact. Here, we consider the generation of impact for REF purposes as a result of work carried out by individual academics and teams. As highlighted in our explanation of the rules underpinning impact submission, only a minority of business school academics are required to get involved in impact work. This gives rise to questions about who belongs to this minority as well as, importantly, whether there are any groups of staff that are in a stronger position than others to generate impact from research and to produce an impact case study. In drawing attention to the existence of such differences, we first focus on the importance of networks for the academic's ability to successfully engage in impact activity. We then elaborate on the structural inequalities affecting different groups of academic staff and influencing their ability to generate research impact outside academia.

4.2 The importance of networks for impact generation

As with the production of REF outputs, the generation of impact directs individual and organisational activities in a certain way. The assessment of impact by REF panels focuses on the strength of evidence which, especially in the case of impact resulting from the work of researchers in business schools and, more broadly, in social sciences disciplines, includes testimonials that confirm and add gravitas to claims about impact. Therefore, the preparation of impact case studies involves a range of stakeholders. For example, to be able to demonstrate that impact on policymaking at a national level has occurred,

DOI: 10.4324/9781003090465-4

the underpinning research needs to have influenced the thinking and decision-making of policymakers, such as Members of Parliament (MPs). Similarly, to be able to show that impact on corporate practice has occurred, it is necessary to present evidence from corporate leaders, attesting that the research has, indeed, led to beneficial changes for the organisation. Here, a question emerges about what makes a piece of research draw the attention of MPs or corporate executives. One answer, of course, lies in the strength of the research itself: the more excellent the research, the more tangible and positive the practical impacts derived from it. In reality, however, other conditions also need to be fulfilled. Every year, a substantial amount of excellent research is published by academics based in business schools and universities across the UK and internationally, but only a very small fraction of this research output gets noticed by national level policymakers and corporate leaders. This suggests that simply conducting and publishing research is not enough, since the researcher(s) whose work has the potential for creating impact outside academia as well as the higher education institution which employs them also must also find themselves on the 'radar' of policymakers and business executives.

As far as making a piece of research noticed by MPs is concerned, it is important not to underestimate the role of networks. Such networks are often forged prior to the research being carried out. Social capital (Bourdieu, 1986) – represented in the higher education context by the personal connections of academics and the institutional connections between certain universities or research units and the Parliament, or, in the case of impact on industry and business, relevant industry and business associations – is crucial for the capacity to attract the attention of decision-makers outside academia. Unsurprisingly, the ability to access and participate in these networks varies among both institutions and academics. In some cases, these differences are associated with the geographical location. For example, business schools based in London are potentially more likely to have established connections with the Westminster Parliament and with other London-based organisations. Analogously, business schools located, e.g. in the North East of England, are more likely to be part of regional and local policy and business networks in that region. The perceived 'prestige' – or cultural capital (Bourdieu, 1986) of the institution matters, too, with renowned universities and business schools being particularly well placed to enter into collaboration with policymakers and key firms. This suggests that academics based in more 'prestigious' and strongly networked institutions might be in a better position than academics from less well-connected business schools to make impact outside academia, even if, as Kellard and Śliwa (2016: 706) argue on the basis of their analysis of REF 2014 impact submissions, 'those organizational contexts that are conducive to generation of "excellent" impact need not be those that are traditionally viewed as "elite" HEIs'.

Belonging to networks also matters as far as an individual academic's ability to engage in collaborative impact work with other researchers is concerned. By its very nature, the generation of impact calls for teamwork: it takes a collective effort to maximise the influence of research on the society and economy. This intuitively obvious observation has been confirmed by Kellard and Śliwa's (2016) analysis of the impact case studies submitted to REF2014 under the Business and Management Unit of Assessment. Methodologically, this involved a three-step procedure. First, conditional on their impact GPA score, 97 institutions were arranged into three clusters (i.e. top, middle, and bottom ranks) using a k-means clustering algorithm. Second, for each cluster and after collecting data from the case studies and institutions, the average value of institution-level variables were calculated including output GPA, number of case studies, number of research outputs listed per case study, percentage of outputs represented by journal articles, listed grant amounts, number of key researchers, percentage of women key researchers, interaction with public and non-profit organisations, and measure of national reach. Third, differences in the average value of institution-level variables *between* the clusters were calculated and examined for any statistical significance using an appropriate distribution. The results from the methodological approach of Kellard and Śliwa (2016) were striking. Successful impact case studies, in the sense of high scores awarded in the REF 2014 exercise, were typically attained by (i) impact teams that consisted of a small group of key researchers, rather than a sole author, (ii) research awarded substantial grant funding, and (iii) academics employed by the institution for a substantial period of time.

Following this logic, it could be expected that impact case studies should be produced by teams of academics working in the same department or institution. However, there is a paradox associated with the generation of impact that takes place in a context of national research evaluation exercises. Such exercises, including the REF, have been shown to drive individualisation of academic work combined with competition among academics (Brooks et al., 2014; Yarrow, 2016). Specifically, with regard to the REF in the UK, it needs to be remembered that the rules underpinning output submission do not incentivise research collaboration with colleagues from the same institution. Compared to single-authored outputs, as well as those resulting from collaboration with academics in other institutions, publications co-authored with colleagues from the same institution might not 'count' for a specific academic due to being 'allocated' to someone else. This aspect of the REF rules is well-established and – even though the majority of business school research is produced in a collaborative way – it encourages academics to seek collaborations with researchers based in other business schools rather than with their own colleagues. This, in turn, poses a challenge as far as the formation of teams for the purposes of preparing REF impact case studies is concerned. In effect, impact case studies end up being authored by both individual academics and teams. At the same time, the potential to become a member of an impact case study team will partly depend on the individual academic's ability to join certain academic networks.

As with business schools' access to stakeholder networks, individual academics' access to both stakeholder and academic networks for the purpose of impact generation – and, more broadly, the ability of an individual researcher to engage in impact activity – is not equally distributed among different groups of academics. In particular, factors such as career stage, gender, ethnicity, nationality, and (dis)ability will influence a person's potential for becoming involved in this type of work. We offer some reflections on these factors in the remainder of this chapter.

4.3 Career stage

One category of academics who are disadvantaged with regard to network access and participation, and therefore also in terms of their ability to produce impact case studies, are early career researchers (ECRs). This is because, in the first place, establishing networks takes time. This requirement, from the outset, disadvantages ECRs who – with the exception of those who enter academia after an earlier career in a sector in which they had previously built strong networks that could be used for impact generation purposes – have not yet had the time to develop professional networks outside academia. Therefore, co-authoring an impact case study by an ECR is unlikely, other than in situations where the early career member of staff gets invited and supported by an established researcher who already is involved in engagement with practice and belongs to a network of relevant stakeholders (Hughes et al., 2019). Such invitations and support, however, should not be taken for granted because, from the perspective of an experienced researcher, the ECR might not have much to 'offer' compared to other, more established academics. Indeed, ECR participation might not be seen as necessary for the production of a successful impact case study. Kellard and Śliwa's (2016) analysis suggests that impact case studies submitted to REF2014, especially those generated within the top ten ranked institutions for business and management impact, were produced by academics who had been embedded for a long time in a given institution: in eight out of the 10 top universities, the average time in service of the longest employed researcher involved in impact generation was 19 years. In addition, established scholars who have developed their networks over a period of many years might not feel the need to reach out to and include early career colleagues in these networks. Therefore, in order for ECRs to become routinely involved in impact generation efforts, a culture change towards greater inclusion of early career staff would be necessary (Hughes et al., 2019).

When considering the potential for ECRs to be involved in research impact generation, it must be remembered that, even when they are part of an impact case study team, early career researchers can be disadvantaged because of what Merton (1968) first referred to as the 'Matthew effect'. In relation to impact generation, the occurrence of the 'Mathew effect' would mean that regardless of the actual contribution of the ECR to the research and the resulting impact, greater credit is likely to be attributed to the person with already existing scientific prestige. In addition, there is an 'opportunity cost' involved in spending time on producing an impact case study, although, of course, this is also the time during which the researcher develops the competencies and skills necessary for impact generation (Hodgkinson et al., 2001; Pettigrew, 2011). For an ECR, due to the institutional prioritisation of the production of REF outputs, dedicating time to impact generation might be risky in terms of their ability to secure permanency and promotion. As Hughes et al. (2019: 637) explain, even if 'the longevity of engagement needed to create impact suggests the need to start early', for ECRs 'the challenge of establishing their own research track, getting published in high-quality journals and teaching already puts a high burden on the individual and engaging with practice on top of this may be very difficult to fit in'. It is important to bear in mind that ECRs are a particularly vulnerable group of academics who face a high degree of pressure and precarity (Robinson et al., 2017), and that the first few years of an academic's career are often a period experienced as one of 'targets and terror' (Ratle et al., 2020). Therefore, meeting REF criteria for publishing research outputs becomes their main objective in the process of securing permanency, and also the dominant preoccupation during the initial years of an ECR's academic employment.

4.4 Gender

Access to impact stakeholder networks and, more broadly, the ability to engage in impact generation, also has a gendered dimension. Existing research demonstrates that academic networks tend to be homosocial and male-dominated (Bagilhole and Goode, 2001; Śliwa and Johansson, 2014). Women, therefore, are less likely to be included in networks of policymakers and industry and business leaders than men, unless these networks' specific remit is oriented towards women, such as, e.g. networks of women entrepreneurs (see Kellard and Śliwa, 2016). Already nearly three decades ago, Rossiter (1993) drew attention to the advantages experienced by men in academia combined with the disadvantages experienced by women. As Rossiter (1993: 337) argued, while male academics benefit from the above-mentioned 'Matthew effect', women tend to find themselves on the receiving end of the 'Matilda effect', whereby their presence in the academic environment as well as their work is systematically under-recognised and ignored. Research also shows that women continue to bear the majority of the burden associated with household and caring responsibilities (Aiston and Jung, 2015; Eisend and Schuchert-Güler, 2015; Tower and Latimer, 2016). The time required for these commitments restricts the time they can spend on developing and maintaining their professional networks, especially those networks that are external to academia.

The disadvantages experienced by women in an academic environment characterised by privileged masculine hegemony (Benschop and Brouns, 2003) translate into reduced opportunities as far as producing impact case studies in concerned. As such, the inclusion of impact measurement as part of UK REF metrics can be considered, along with other HE policy metrics, problematic in terms of its effect on women scholars' career progression and ways of working (Knights and Richards, 2003; Yarrow, 2016). Davies et al.'s (2020) analysis of the authorship of REF 2014 Business and Management impact case studies shows that only 25% of REF 2014 impact case studies were led or co-led by women, and that 54% of these had women as sole authors, indicating that where women did engage in impact work, they did it on their own rather than as part of a team of researchers. Davies et al. (2020: 138) describe this situation as an 'impoverished model without a team of academics supporting research impact efforts'. It is also worth noting that impact case studies produced by women researchers were evaluated as being of a lower quality than those produced by men. According to Kellard and Śliwa's (2016) analysis, in the 'bottom 10' cluster of institutions within the ranking of business and management REF2014 impact, nearly half of the impact case study authors were women. Moreover, the authors found that among the three clusters of institutions – 'top', 'middle', and 'bottom' 10 – 'while it was rather common for impact case studies to be built around the work of a team of three or more, there was only one case study amongst those submitted by the 30 institutions within the three analysed clusters where all three key researchers on the team were women' (Kellard and Śliwa, 2016: 708).

In discussing the reasons behind women's underrepresentation as authors of impact case studies, Davies et al. (2020) point to path- and status-dependent cumulative disadvantage (Cole and Singer, 1991) experienced by women, which persists, regardless of the, by now many, years of organisational policies ostensibly aimed at countering these disadvantages. Conceptually, Davies et al. (2020) locate the issue of women's participation in the generation of research impact outside academia with reference to Acker's (2006: 443) notion of workplace inequality regimes, that is:

> Systematic disparities between participants in power and control over goals, resources, and outcomes; workplace decisions such as how to organize work; opportunities for promotion and interesting work; security in employment and benefits; pay and other monetary rewards; respect and pleasures in work and work relations.

These systematic disparities are gendered because organisations operate 'on the assumption that the ordinary worker is a man, an abstract person who has few obligations outside work that could distract him from the centrality of work' (Acker, 1998: 197). Such assumptions regarding the ability to be in charge of one's time and to put work at the centre of one's life are particularly pronounced in relation to the generation of impact. This is because there is often an expectation that impact-related work, which involves a range of activities and networking with parties outside one's workplace organisation, should be carried out above and beyond the academic's day-to-day responsibilities and workload. In other words, engagement in research impact generation is more realistic for someone who is in the position to dedicate long uninterrupted hours to work than for someone who is not able to do this due to responsibilities outside work, such as caring commitments. On the other hand, having no or few responsibilities outside work continues to be more likely for men than for women (Aiston and Jung, 2015). As a result, men continue to benefit from gendered privilege in academia, and the low representation of women as impact case studies authors can be seen as evidence of this, along with other examples of evidence such as gender pay disparity (Pells, 2019) or HESA (2020) data showing that 76% of professors in UK business and management schools are men, even though around half of all UK business school faculty are women (Metz et al., 2016).

Another aspect of gendered inequality that is likely to affect women's participation in the generation of research impact is associated with women's engagement in 'academic housework' which tends to be higher than men's engagement in this type of work (Heijstra et al., 2017; Macfarlane and Burg, 2019). The idea of 'academic housework' refers to 'women taking on gendered responsibilities associated with caring in the workplace that can result in an excessive amount of time-consuming and lowly esteemed service work' (Macfarlane and Burg, 2019: 264). Whilst existing research suggests that 'academic housework' negatively affects women's research productivity and leads to delaying or even prohibiting chances for promotion (Grant and Knowles, 2000; Misra et al., 2011; Macfarlane and Burg, 2019), in the context of impact generation it is important to see it also as resulting in lowering a person's capacity to engage in impact work. When attention, energy, and time are focused on contributing to one's employment organisation, it is unsurprising that a similar level of activities outside academia, such as those associated with impact generation, will simply not occur. Davies et al.'s (2020) study confirmed that women in particular lack the necessary time and resources, within their allocated workloads, to engage with the research impact agenda.

The currently existing gendered 'division of labour' evident in the distinction between 'academic housework' that occurs inside the organisation, and is carried out primarily by women, and impact work that takes places outside it, and is conducted primarily by men, gives rise to interesting connotations with the division of labour and gender power relations in traditional societies. It brings to mind a parallel with hunter-gatherer communities, with men-hunters having greater power, control, and prestige, because of being in the position to provide the community with a desirable good obtained outside the community, i.e. animal protein, and women-gatherers having less power, control, and prestige, despite the enormous work they carry out within the community. As the anthropologist Ernestine Friedl (1978) observed several decades ago based on her research on hunter-gatherer societies, the higher the proportion of meat supplied by men, the higher the extent of male dominance. This parallel is worth bearing in mind in the context of gender inequalities that can be observed in relation to impact generation because it points to how overall gender inequalities in academia are further exacerbated by men academics' disproportionately higher participation in impact activities. What is also worth remembering is that women themselves might opt out of impact generation work. As Śliwa and Johansson's (2014) study has demonstrated, women academics do not only get excluded by others but can also self-exclude from participating in those professional activities that are considered to be of high value by universities.

The inclusion of evaluation of impact as part of research assessment audits has led to the emergence of new 'modalities of scholarly distinction' (Watermeyer and Chubb, 2019), which nevertheless are characterised by old patterns of gender inequalities. Those who produce impact, accrue through it additional prestige compared to those who do not, despite the fact that without the work of the latter group the organisation would not be able to function. Ironically, then, the introduction of impact measurement results in women's position in academia becoming even less powerful than before, regardless of how high their contribution to the organisation is, as reflected in women's typically, and sometimes unfairly, high workload allocations (Barrett and Barrett, 2011). In the experience of Davies et al.'s (2020: 138) study participants, business schools operate according to cultural norms set by men, and within these cultures, 'it appears to be the norm for some men... to appropriate impact to display political capital', sometimes even in cases where impact was generated by women. As Acker (2006: 457) reminds us: 'inequality becomes a sign of success for those who win'. By contrast, women researchers in Davies et al.'s (2020: 140) study appeared to be 'less forceful' than men in terms of 'selling their own contributions in the impact agenda' and seemed to 'lack the self-promotion and bravado of men in the same position'. In addition, the actual writers of impacts cases, i.e. professional service staff whose task it was to draft the impact case studies were also often women, and they worked 'behind the scenes' preparing case studies for men academics. All this builds a picture of impact generation as a sphere of academic work within which, at present, women are disadvantaged compared to men.

4.5 Nationality, ethnicity, and race

The differences between different groups of academics in terms of their ability to engage in impact activity also need to be acknowledged in relation to nationality and ethnicity. For example, due to the homosociality of stakeholder networks, British-born researchers are better placed to access these networks than non-UK born staff. This is particularly important in the case of business schools, which in the UK tend to be highly internationalised (HESA, 2020). In attempting to forge links with national-level policymakers and industry leaders, international academics are likely to encounter cultural and linguistic barriers. On the other hand, potentially, academics who arrived in the UK from other countries – especially those who come from social elite backgrounds which equipped them with the social capital necessary to have an influence in business and government circles – can access and take advantage of stakeholder networks which they had developed in their countries of origin. Unfortunately, we are not able to provide an analysis of the nationality of impact case study authors based on empirical data but, for reasons mentioned above, we expect nationality to influence the probability of an academic engaging in impact generation. Especially, we expect that it is less likely for non-UK born academics to be authors of impact case studies demonstrating impact on UK policy and on British businesses.

Similarly, we do not have access to data that would allow us to examine the link between ethnicity and engagement in impact generation. The lack of such data in itself suggests that having a picture of the nationality- and ethnicity-related dimension of REF impact generation is not a priority for HE policymakers in the UK. However, it is important not to ignore the fact that since 'racism and discrimination continue to persist in the UK and globally' (Bhopal and Pitkin, 2020: 530), race and ethnicity can be expected to have an influence on an academic's ability to produce impact. The emergence of initiatives, such as Race Equality Charter (see also Advance HE, 2018a, 2018b), combined with continued experiences of racism among BAME staff and students (Trade Unions Council (TUC), 2017; Social Market Foundation/UPP, 2018) point to the existence of racially based inequalities within UK academia. Specifically, with reference to business schools, Dar et al. (2021) claim unambiguously that 'the business school is racist'. The most disadvantaged group among all BAME staff are black people: across UK academia, 91.6% of all professors are white and just 0.6%

are black (Advance HE, 2018a). Viewing these statistics through the lens of Critical Race Theory (CRT) reminds us that 'racism is a normal part of daily life in society and that the assumptions of White superiority are deeply ingrained in political, legal and educational structures' (Bhopal and Pitkin, 2020: 533). Moreover, research has shown that so far, efforts aimed at addressing inequalities in higher education have been privileging gender over race (Bhopal and Henderson, 2021). It can therefore be expected that impact generation – and the prestige and rewards associated with being the author of an impact case study – are not equally distributed among academic staff from different ethnicities working in business schools.

4.6 The importance of other dimensions of diversity

We have argued above that a range of circumstances associated with different aspects of diversity among academics, such as type of institution, career stage, gender, nationality, ethnicity, and race will influence whether and to what extent a person is in the position to become part of relevant academic and external stakeholder networks and to engage in impact generation. Of course, there are also other dimensions of diversity which have the potential to influence an individual researcher's ability to produce research impact outside academia. In this context it is important to remember that The Public Sector Equality Duty, which is part of the Equality Act (2010), requires all British universities to promote diversity in their day-to-day business. The Act distinguishes between nine 'protected characteristics': age, disability, gender reassignment, marriage and civil partnership, pregnancy and maternity, race, religion or belief, sex, and sexual orientation. In adhering to the Equality Act, universities are legally obliged to 'have due regard to the need to:

- Eliminate unlawful discrimination, harassment and victimisation and other conduct prohibited by the Act;
- Advance equality of opportunity between people who share a protected characteristic and those who do not;
- Foster good relations between people who share a protected characteristic and those who do not' (equalityhumanrights.com).

The notion of 'having due regard for advancing equality involves:

- Removing or minimising disadvantages suffered by people due to their protected characteristics;
- Taking steps to meet the needs of people from protected groups where these are different from the needs of other people;
- Encouraging people from protected groups to participate in public life or in other activities where their participation is low' (equalityhumantights.com).

The obligation to fulfil Public Sector Equality Duty means that if we see impact generation as integral to the day-to-day business of universities, then we must also be mindful of the broad range of inequalities underpinning the production of impact as well as those resulting from it, and to be able to consider them with reference to the nine protected characteristics. In addition, we should also be aware that the experiences and achievements of academics – including those related to impact generation – will be influenced by the intersections of more than one aspect of diversity operating simultaneously (Nichols and Stahl, 2019).

4.7 Conclusion

In this chapter, we have discussed how the ability to engage in impact generation is unevenly distributed among researchers. In doing so, we have pointed to structural inequalities along the lines of career stage, gender, nationality, ethnicity, and race. We have also signalled the need to pay attention to other aspects of diversity, as outlined in the Equality Act (2010), and to intersections of these, as significant for a person's ability to produce impact. What emerges from the above discussion is that to answer the question about who generates, for the purposes of research quality audits, research impact outside academia, it is necessary to move beyond reference to ideas rooted in meritocratic principles (see Śliwa and Johansson, 2014), such as 'outstanding researchers' or 'researchers who have produced outstanding research'. As all organisations constitute a 'microcosm' of the broader society, impact generation will inevitably be characterised by the same patterns of inequalities and exclusions that can be observed in society at large (see Contu, 2020). Building upon the discussion presented here, in the next chapter we will elaborate on the myriad intended and unintended consequences of impact generation, understood as a set of organisational processes and practices, for business schools and for individual academics.

References

Abreu, M. and Grinevich, V. (2013) The nature of academic entrepreneurship in the UK: Widening the focus on entrepreneurial activities. *Research Policy*, 42 (2), 408–422.

Acker, J. (1998) The future of 'gender and organisations': Connections and boundaries. *Gender, Work and Organization*, 5 (4), 195–206.

Acker, J. (2006) Inequality regimes: Gender, class, and race in organizations. *Gender & Society*, 20 (4), 441–464.

Advance HE (2018a) *Staff statistical report*. London: Advance HE.

Advance HE (2018b) *Students statistical report*. London: Advance HE.

Aiston, S.J. and Jung, J. (2015) Women academics and research productivity: An international comparison. *Gender and Education*, 27 (3), 205–220.

Bagilhole, B. and Goode, J. (2001) The contradiction of the myth of individual merit, and the reality of a patriarchal support system in cademic areers. *The European Journal of Women's Studies*, 8 (2), 161–180.

Barrett, L. and Barrett, P. (2011) Women and academic workloads: Career slow lane or cul-de-sac? *Higher Education*, 61 (2), 141–155.

Benschop, Y. and Brouns, M. (2003) Crumbling ivory towers: Academic organizing and its gender effects. *Gender, Work and Organization*, 10 (2), 194–212.

Bhopal, K. and Henderson, H. (2021) Competing inequalities: Gender versus race in higher education institutions in the UK. *Education Review*, 73 (2), 153–161.

Bhopal, K. and Pitkin, C. (2020) 'Same old story, just a different policy': Race and policy making in higher education in the UK. *Race Ethnicity and Education*, 23 (4), 530–547.

Bourdieu, P. (1986) The forms of capital. *In*: Richardson, J., ed. *Handbook of theory and research for the sociology of education*. Westport, CT: Greenwood, 241–258.

Brooks, C., Fenton, E. and Walker, J. (2014) Gender and the evaluation of research. *Research Policy*, 43 (6), 990–1001.

Cole, J.R. and Singer, B. (1991) A theory of limited differences: Explaining the productivity puzzle in science. *In*: H. Zuckerman, J.R. Cole, and J.T. Bruer, eds. *The outer circle: Women in the scientific community*. New York, NY: W. W. Norton, 277–310.

Contu, A. (2020) Answering the crisis with intellectual activism: Making a difference as business school scholars. *Human Relations*, 73 (5), 737–757.

Dar, S., et al. (2021) The business school is racist: Act up! *Organization*, 28 (4), 695–706.

Davies, J., Yarrow, E. and Syed, J. (2020) The curious under-representation of women impact case leaders: Can we disengender inequality regimes? *Gender, Work and Organization*, 27 (2), 129–148.

Eisend, M. and Schuchert-Güler, P. (2015) Journal publication success of German business researchers: Does gender composition and internationality of the author team matter? *Business Research*, 8 (2), 171–188.

Equality Act   (2010) https://www.legislation.gov.uk/ukpga/2010/15/contents. Accessed on 25 March 2021.

Friedl, E. (1978) Society and sex roles. *Human Nature*, 1, 100–104.

Grant, B. and Knowles, S. (2000) Flights of imagination: Academic women be(com)ing writers. *International Journal for Academic Development*, 5 (1), 6–19.

Heijstra, T. M., Steinthorsdóttir, F.S. and Einarsdóttir, T. (2017) Academic career making and the double-edged role of academic housework. *Gender and Education*, 29 (6), 764–780.

HESA. (2020) Higher education staff statistics: UK, 2019/20. https://www.hesa.ac.uk/news/24-01-2019/sb253-higher-education-staff-statistics. Accessed on 25 March 2021.

Hodgkinson, G.P., Herriot, P., and Anderson, N. (2001) Re-aligning the stakeholders in management research: Lessons from industrial, work and organizational psychology. *British Journal of Management*, 12 (1), 41–48.

Hughes, T., Webber, D., and O'Regan, N. (2019) Achieving wider impact in business and management: Analysing case studies from REF 2014. *Studies in Higher Education*, 44 (4), 628–642.

Kellard, N.M. and Śliwa, M. (2016) Business and management impact assessment in REF2014: Analysis and reflection. *British Journal of Management*, 27 (4), 693–711.

Knights, D. and Richards, W. (2003) Sex discrimination in UK academia. *Gender, Work and Organization*, 10 (2), 213–238.

Macfarlane, B. and Burg, D. (2019) Women professors and the academic housework trap. *Journal of Higher Education Policy and Management*, 41 (3), 262–274.

Merton, R. K. (1968) The Matthew Effect in science. *Science*, 159, 56–63.

Metz, I., Harzing, A.-W. and Zyphur, M.J. (2016) Of journal editors and editorial boards: Who are the trailblazers in increasing editorial board gender equality? *British Journal of Management*, 27 (4), 712–726.

Misra, J., Lundquist, J.H., Holmes, E. and Agiomavritis, S. (2011) The ivory ceiling of service work. *Academe*, 97 (1), 22.

Nichols, S. and Stahl, G. (2019) Intersectionality in higher education research: A systematic literature review. *Higher Education Research and Development*, 38 (6), 1255–1268.

Pells, R. (2019) Gender pay gap: UK universities report slow progress, *Times Higher Education*, 8th April. https://www.timeshighereducation.com/news/gender-pay-gap-uk-universities-report-slow-progress. Accessed 25 March 2021.

Pettigrew, A.M. (2011) Viewpoint: Scholarship with impact. *British Journal of Management*, 22 (3), 347–354.

Ratle, O., Robinson, S. and Bristow, A. (2020) Mechanisms of micro-terror? Early career CMS academics' experiences of "targets and terror" in contemporary business schools. *Management Learning*, 51 (4), 452–471.

Robinson, S., Ratle, O. and Bristow, A. (2017) Labour pains: Starting a career within the neo-liberal university. *Ephemera. Theory and Politics in Organization*, 17 (3), 481–508.

Rossiter, M. (1993) The Matthew Matilda Effect in science. *Social Studies of Science*, 23 (1), 325–341.

Shapiro, D.L., Kirkman, B.L. and Courtney, H.G. (2007) Perceived causes and solutions of the translation problem in Management Research. *Academy of Management Journal*, 50 (2), 249–266.

Śliwa, M. and Johansson, M. (2014) The discourse of meritocracy contested/ reproduced: Foreign women academics in UK business schools. *Organization*, 21 (6), 821–843.

Social Market Foundation/UPP (2018) On course for success? *Student retention at university*. London: SMF/UPP.

Tower, L.E. and Latimer, M. (2016) Cumulative disadvantage: Effects of early career childcare issues on faculty research travel. *Affilia*, 31 (3), 317–330.

Trade Unions Council (TUC). (2017) *Is Racism Real?* London: TUC.

Watermeyer, R. and Chubb, J. (2019) Evaluating 'impact' in the UK'S Research Excellence Framework (REF): Liminality, looseness and new modalities of scholarly distinction. *Studies in Higher Education*, 44 (9), 1554–1566.

Yarrow, E. (2016) National research evaluation and its effects on female academics' careers in the UK: A case study (Unpublished PhD thesis).

5 The (un)intended consequences of impact: university, society, and economy

5.1 Introduction

In the previous chapter, we focused on the 'impact' of impact, particularly with respect to different groups of academics on the basis of different aspects of diversity. Amongst other things, we highlighted that the current impact process as constituted under UK Research Excellence Framework (REF) rules and guidelines, results in problematic, exclusionary outcomes for women, early career researchers, and – very likely – members of other minority groups. In this current chapter, we discuss the intended and perhaps unintended consequences of impact from a meso- and macro-perspective, considering effects at the level of the business school, the university, and the local, national, and international society and economy.

A good starting place for this discussion are the reports prepared for HEFCE by Rand Europe (see Manville et al., 2015a, 2015b) that provide a first widescale evaluation of the impact process under REF 2014. Adopting a mixed-methods approach – including site visits, interviews, online surveys, and cost estimation – the authors sample 21 UK HEIs and focus on three primary groups: senior university managers, impact case study writers, and non-academic research users. Amongst other things, Manville et al. (2015a) stress the following findings:

- Participants suggested benefits included 'the ability to identify and understand impact; the stimulation of broader strategic thinking about impact; the increased recognition within HEIs of those academics undertaking impact activities; and the opportunity to review and reaffirm relationships with external stakeholders' (Manville et al., 2015a: xii). However, these positive views were concentrated in groupings overseeing a University's impact process, rather than the wider academic community.

DOI: 10.4324/9781003090465-5

- There is a resulting cultural shift occurring in UK HEIs which are now explicitly addressing impact as part of strategic aims and developing operational processes to achieve these aims at both a University and a Departmental/School level.
- There was widespread concern that the impact case studies selected did not fully represent the extent of the impact research was having in non-academic settings. In part, this stems from uncertainty within HEIs over the eligibility of certain case studies under the current guidance. Relatedly, there was concern that research that was more easily 'evidenced' in terms of impact, may crowd out less easily evidenced or more 'blue skies' research.
- The financial cost to HEIs of the impact process itself is substantial. Specifically, the total cost to UK HEIs was estimated at £55m (*ibid.*: xii) with the median cost of a single case study given as £7,500. The authors noted some economies of scale effects benefitting larger HEIs.

Overall, Manville et al. (2015a) conclude that the REF 2014 exercise successfully allowed UK HEIs to articulate their research impact but that the longer-term effectiveness of the framework would depend on (i) value for money considerations and (ii) continuing cultural change and therefore, its acceptance within the wider academic community. In our view, the inclusion of impact within the REF certainly allowed universities to both showcase the effect of research in many non-academic contexts, including the economy, and demonstrate that such effects are significant, positive, and multidimensional. This perspective is corroborated by the scores given for impact in REF 2014, when UK HEIs submitted a total of 6,975 case studies[1] across the 36 Units of Assessment (UoAs). Table 5.1 and Figure 5.1 present an overview of the impact scores awarded.

As calculated in Kellard and Śliwa (2016), Table 5.1 reveals that the mean average FTE-adjusted impact GPA for the 36 UoAs was 3.21. This judges the average case study to have produced between 'outstanding' and 'very considerable' impacts in relation to their reach and significance.[2]

Table 5.1 FTE-adjusted Impact GPA for all Units

	Mean	*Standard Deviation*	*Maximum*	*Minimum*
Impact GPA	3.21	0.15	3.71	2.99

Notes: Reproduced from Kellard and Śliwa (2016).

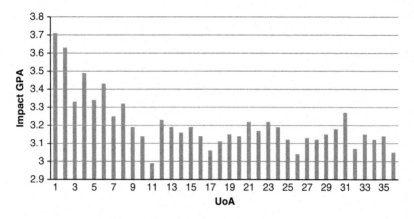

Figure 5.1 FTE-adjusted Impact GPA by UoA.

Notes: Reproduced from Kellard and Śliwa (2016).

Interestingly, there was some variance between the average scores. Figure 5.1 provides a histogram of the average impact GPA for all UoAs, and as pointed out by Kellard and Śliwa (2016), the social sciences, humanities, and the arts (i.e., UoAs 17-36) typically have lower averages than the sciences (i.e. UoAs 1-16). There were some notable exceptions to this trend though; most strikingly, computer science (UoA 11) obtained the lowest average impact GPA of 2.99.

The 432 impact case studies, the most for any UoA, submitted for business and management studies (UoA 19)[3] also scored well and with average FTE-adjusted impact GPA of 3.15, just below the mean for all units. Indeed, the overview report provided by Main Panel C for UoA 19 commented, 'It is pleasing that a large majority of submissions showed elements of outstanding impact and clear relevance to policy or practice or both' (REF, 2015: 56) and, when considering the distribution of scores shown in Figure 5.2 noted, 'Half or more of the impact work described in almost 30 per cent of submissions was rated as outstanding, which is a real credit to those institutions and to the field of business and management studies' (*ibid.*: 57).

As discussed in Chapter 3, the assessment of impact can be seen as driven by the wish that universities demonstrate their *use value* to government. Despite this being, at best, a very partial 'accounting' treatment for impact, universities in general and their business schools have provided a convincing case for the influence of their research outside the academic context. However, it is important to ask: at what cost?

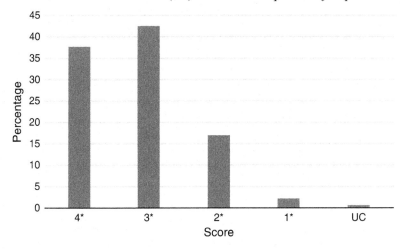

Figure 5.2 Weighted average impact profile for UoA 19.
Notes: Source is REF (2015).

In purely financial terms, as we note above, Manville et al. (2015a) suggest the additional assessment of impact cost UK HEIs £55m. This non-trivial amount has opportunity costs, approximately representing the annual undergraduate home fees bursary for almost 6,000 students or employment for over 1,000 new lecturers. Moreover, aside from assuring government that impact is occurring, it is far from clear whether the exercise itself is merely accounting for a small proportion of impact that universities generate or that the process itself stimulates further impact. If simply the former, and given the financial cost of the exercise, one would have to wonder about purpose of repeating the impact component in any future REF. Such doubts are compounded by questions including concerns that the impact exercise itself crowds out other valuable activities including teaching, maintains or enhances structural divisions between UK HEIs, and privileges certain types of impact over others. We investigate these issues in the following sections.

5.2 The crowded-out university

A common feature of academic life, and in particular, academic life in the UK, is the culture and practice of overwork. A recent survey (see Erickson et al., 2020) of almost 6,000 UK-based academics, eliciting views on senior management practices and university governance, revealed striking concerns about workload and related issues. Upon analysing the survey results, the researchers concluded:

> The qualitative data that the SMS [senior management survey] collected reveal an acute situation of endemic bullying and harassment, chronic overwork, high levels of mental health problems, general health and wellbeing problems, and catastrophically high levels of demoralisation and dissatisfaction across the UK HE sector. This suggests that a sector that is vitally important for the UK knowledge economy is on the edge of potential disaster (Erickson et al., 2020: 15).

Using the survey, and in a reversal of the typical top-down approach to construction, Erickson et al. (2020) produced a university league table of academics' satisfaction with management as an aid to bring about change in HEI governance.

Other evidence of excessive workloads and long working hours in academia can be found in analogous surveys. For example, Wellcome (2020), based on a sample of over 4,000 researchers predominantly based in the UK and at HEIs stress that '57% of respondents agreed that there was a long-hours working culture at their workplace, while 48% agreed that they had felt pressured to work long hours. Furthermore, 62% agreed that the system exploited their interest in the work, leading to a heavy workload' (Wellcome, 2020: 34). In terms of average hours worked, 40% of respondents were in the 41–50 hours per week category, whilst a striking 32% were working over 50 hours per week. For many academics, this overwork is rooted in the proliferation of audit within the sector, with work such as Ratle et al. (2020: 453) using attention-grabbing concepts such as 'targets and terror' in their attempt 'to problematise the audit culture within universities (...) and specifically business schools', a culture which leads to anxiety (Hall and Bowles, 2016), other mental health issues (Ruth et al., 2018) and poor well-being. Indeed, Ratle et al.'s (2020) conceptual framework, in addition to the external pressures from audit, also includes the important notion that academics 'micro-terrorise themselves'; in other words, as well as being overly pressured by excessive external targets, some academics respond by attempting to adhere to unrealistic workloads and expectations, at the expense of their well-being.

As discussed in Chapter 4, workload has a gendered dimension, with women more likely to be engaged in academic housework (Macfarlane and Burg, 2019) and also more likely to have outside work commitments (Aiston and Jung, 2015). As corollary then, if overwork is the experience of the average contemporary academic, the marginal burden is likely to fall more on women than men. Given the empirical evidence of excessive workloads and the equality duty of public bodies (see the Equality Act, 2010, section 149), it makes it even more surprising – and deserving of a comprehensive reflection – that an additional audit, in this case, impact assessment, has been introduced with little consideration of either the overall 'impact' on workloads or the gendered distribution of additional tasks. As a consequence, there would also appear to be limited consideration about which current tasks the impact accounting mechanism may displace and/or damage. Indeed, one might conclude worryingly, that there would appear to be no 'portfolio thinking' from HE policy-makers, just the unspoken assumption that more siloed tasks can simply be added.

The lack of attention to, and planning of, the potential workload implications relating to the introduction of the impact assessment mechanism, may be due to several reasons. Of course, one cannot rule out neglect and the related convenience of not having to acknowledge that those working in the HE sector have finite resources. As a conceptual framing, some may see 'audit' as inherently reasonable and required, something that should always be accommodated. However, there are 'real-life', tangible consequences of adding another assessment. Again, as we saw earlier in Chapter 4, work such as Anderson et al. (2017) underlines that academic activities (e.g. teaching, research, impact, mentoring, administration, consultancy, advocation, and policy advice) should not be viewed separately from one another. Additional tasks will clearly have an effect both on the aggregate workload and on the focus that other activities can receive, and this is particularly the case given many in the sector seem close to or experiencing burnout (Fazackerley, 2019; GeLashuel, 2020).

5.3 The trapped university

A major critique of the measurement and audit approach to assessing education per se, and university and management education more specifically, is derived from the production of league tables. In the HE sector, rankings such as *The Times* 'Good University Guide' employ the institutional profiles awarded in the REF as a weighted component in their overall measure. Indeed, in *The Times'* methodology, research quality (from the REF) and student satisfaction (based on the National Student Survey or NSS) are relatively overweighted at 1.5, whilst other inputs including entry standards, graduate prospects, proportions of firsts and 2:1s, completion rates, staff-student ratio, and services and facilities spend are weighted 1 (see *The Times*, 2020).[4] On the specific calculation of research quality, *The Times* only takes into account 4* and 3* work as classified by the REF panel; 2* and 1* work are given a zero weighting.

There are many other university league tables and ranking systems including the QS World University Rankings, the Complete University Guide, and, in the context of Business Schools, the *Financial Times* (*FT*) Global MBA ranking. Several universities target improved performance in such tables as a key performance indicator. However, work such as Wedlin (2011) argues that rankings can lead to a 'preservation of status'. In particular, Wedlin (2011) uses institutional theory to propose that 'rankings function as rhetorical devices to construct legitimacy within the field, which actors use to attempt to shape and reform the field as it develops' (Wedlin 2011: 200). Employing a qualitative approach to study the effect of the introduction of the *FT* ranking in 1999 and drawing on Bourdieu's (1984) concept of habitus, Wedlin (2011: 213–214) also argues that:

> 'the construction of new measurement systems are guided to a significant extent by existing structures, positions and principles' and 'precedence is given to dominating and high-status actors and their perspective in the rankings, as these come to take on important roles in the development and legitimation of these systems'.

In this sense, rankings lead to the preservation, and even the further embedding, of the hierarchical status quo in the university sector rather than facilitating contestation. Universities can become trapped in the widely known viewpoint given by the rankings, a viewpoint that legitimises the current ordering and as Green (2004) and Green et al. (2009) posit, is underpinned by taken-for-granted (Zucker, 1977) assumptions.

One quantitative approach to investigate whether the above theory holds in relation to the introduction of impact assessment, would be to assess how similar the impact scores or associated ranks from REF 2014 are to more established measures, including research output. For example, Kellard and Śliwa (2016) examine the association between impact and output GPA scores for UoA 19 business and management studies.

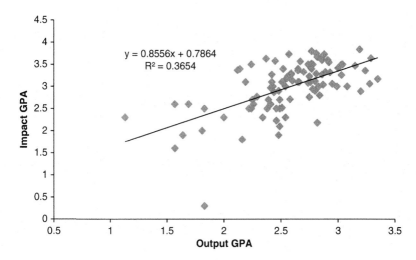

Figure 5.3 Impact and output GPA for UoA 19.

Notes: Reproduced from Kellard and Śliwa (2016).

Figure 5.3 shows the scatter plot of both scores and the super-imposing of the least-squares line of best fit and associated R^2. As Kellard and Śliwa (2016: 699) comment, the positive slope of this line is 'suggesting that at least to some extent those institutions with higher output GPAs were more likely to receive higher grades for impact'. This certainly provides some evidence that impact scores are unlikely to substantially overturn pre-existing measures of research quality. Given we are most concerned with rankings, perhaps an even more appropriate calculation though would be some rank-based correlation, which would also be robust to non-normality in the underlying scores. Converting the data in Figure 5.3 to a rank-based order, provides a Spearman rank correlation of 0.56, indicative of a strongly positive association between impact and output rankings.

On the other hand, the Spearman measure is not signalling that the orderings are entirely similar. For example, as reported by Kellard and Śliwa (2016), the top 10 institutions for impact included two post-1992 universities, the University of Brighton and Bournemouth University. Eyeballing the top thirty institutions for impact locates five post-1992 universities, adding the University of Portsmouth, Coventry University, and the University of Huddersfield to the two aforementioned cases. For comparison, note that there were no post-1992 universities in the top 30 institutions for research output. However, given the weighting for impact will increase in REF 2021 only marginally from 20% in 2014 to 25% (REF 01.2019:7), with a commensurate decrease in the weighting on research output from 65% to 60%, there is only a limited possibility of some challenge to the conventional orderings in the business and management field.

5.4 The connected university

As noted in the introduction to this chapter, in their survey work for Rand Europe on behalf of HEFCE, Manville et al. (2015a) found that many academics were concerned that the impact case studies submitted to REF 2014 were not representative of the impact work carried out by the UoA. In one arresting quote, a respondent commented: 'It is a sliver of what impact actually is going on. There is still a lot of other impact work that we do which wasn't included' (Manville et al., 2015a: 24). There were two stand-out reasons for this highlighted by the survey. The first involved uncertainty around the definition of impact itself and whether certain types of case studies were permitted, specifically:

> These included, but were not limited to, impact case studies relating to public engagement, those with impacts on HEI practice and teaching, and those that included work undertaken by PhD students. It was felt that the eligibility rules led to the first two of these areas being perceived as 'riskier' because there were more applicable caveats in the guidance (*ibid*: 26).

The second reason involved the difficulties in obtaining the necessary evidence to link the underpinning research to the impact claims. Such challenges stemmed in part from both concerns over confidentiality from research users, and also from obtaining testimonials from users who have either moved to different departments within the same organisation or even moved to a separate company.

The above sentiments lead to the question of whether the impact exercise itself favoured certain broader types of impact over others. For example, it would seem that HEI practice and teaching are likely to be underrepresented in the case studies submitted given concerns over eligibility. Furthermore, there would seem to be a *prima facie* case that impact case studies would be drawn more from public sector organisations, other than HEIs, rather than private sector users of academic research. This is particularly so given issues of movements of staff and confidentiality might be more acute in the private sector. A recent report by the Office of National Statistics (see Office of National Statistics, 2019) found that the 1-year retention rate for many careers in the public sector (e.g. local and national government administrative roles, doctors, nurses and midwives, police) was higher than the UK workforce and private sector average. In addition, it is quite possible that the average firm in the private sector is prone to culture less open to sharing, and more prone to secrecy and consequently, are characterised by more requirements around confidentiality. As the Rand Europe report emphasised:

> Quantitative data were especially difficult to access, in particular confidential and sensitive commercial information regarding sales, revenues and figures about expanding markets, and new product lines. This concern may apply to many industries, but specific ones mentioned during our site visits were the pharmaceutical sector, trade publishers and oil, gas, and mineral exploration industries (Manville et al., 2015a: 17).

Of course, whether impact case studies selected in the REF were drawn more from public sector research users, excluding HEIs, is ultimately an empirical question. Kellard and Śliwa (2016), in their analysis of the REF 2014 impact case studies, submitted by HEIs to UoA 19 business and management studies, employed a k-means clustering approach to group HEIs by impact GPA. After computing top-, middle-, and bottom-scoring clusters of HEIs, the values of potential explanatory factors were collected for each clustered HEI including research output GPA, number of case studies, listed grant amounts associated with case studies, years in post for longest serving key researcher, percentage of women key researchers, proportion of case studies associated with public and non-profit organisations, and proportion of case studies where impact occurred only within a single country. The latter two factors, termed 'percent public' and 'percent national reach', were acquired from an in-depth reading of each case study.

Kellard and Śliwa (2016) found that average value of 'percent public' across the three clusters was 71.5%, 66.3%, and 83.3% for the top, middle, and bottom groupings, respectively. In other words, as theorised above, there is evidence that majority of case studies submitted (at least within business and management studies), disseminated impact in the public sector as opposed to private companies. In addition to the reasons already outlined, Kellard and Śliwa (2016: 709) suggest that:

It might also be that the REF 2014 rules, which required the research underpinning impact to be of at least 'two star' quality, made it difficult for many business schools, especially those based in post-1992 universities, to showcase their long established engagement with industry and their influence on management and organizational practice through the work of those staff who are active in applied research and knowledge transfer activity but do not focus on publication of research outputs.

The omission of impact characterised by strong, ongoing ties between universities and other organisations, whilst being underpinned by a wider understanding of research than currently allowed for in the REF, further compromises the representativeness of the impact exercise and, returning to the issues raised in Section 5.3 around university league tables, appears likely to privilege older universities whilst suppressing the potential for positive movements in current university rankings for newer HEIs.

For this chapter and drawing on the same UoA 19 cases studies examined by Kellard and Śliwa (2016), we assessed the number of case studies that involved HEI practice and teaching; strikingly, only one case study in the top-, middle-, or bottom clusters (covering 30 HEIs and 104 case studies) involved HEI-related impact. Indeed, across 410 case studies[5] in UoA 19, only 35 were classified as pertaining to education research. However, compared to other UoAs, this almost 9% of case studies is a relatively high proportion.

Figure 5.4 provides a histogram of the number of education-research–related case studies for all UoAs, showing that whilst not particularly sizable, the number of these case studies in UoA 19 business and management studies was higher than any other UoA, when leaving aside UoA 25 education.[6] Indeed, the figure reveals that across the entire REF 2014 exercise, very few education-related impact case studies were submitted. In fact, they totalled 193, compared to 6422 non-UoA 25 case studies, clearly demonstrating that HEI practice and teaching was underrepresented and bringing into sharp relief the comment of an interviewee in the Rand Europe report that 'the assumption that research-led teaching doesn't have an impact is a large omission' (Manville et al., 2015a: 26). Combining this absence with the relative lack of case studies involving the private sector, suggests that whilst the current case study mechanism has allowed universities to showcase some excellent work, it largely underplays the diversity of HEI impact and connectedness.

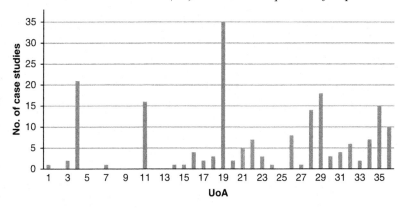

Figure 5.4 Number of education-research case studies by UoA.

Notes: Source is https://impact.ref.ac.uk/casestudies/. This figure excludes the data for UoA 25 Education.

5.5 The stretched university

Another dimension of university connectedness is its geographical reach and influence. How easy was it for HEIs to demonstrate and evidence reach for REF 2014? Certainly, the Rand Europe report casts doubt on whether evidencing international impact is a straightforward endeavour, pointing out that 'Contacting international research users was a particular challenge. One interviewee said that research users outside the UK were "almost impossible to get hold of, do not keep statistics nor understand the value of doing so"' (Manville et al., 2015b: 17). Kellard and Śliwa (2016) investigated this question from another angle, calculating the proportion of case studies where impact occurred only within a single country, termed 'percent national reach', for each of their clustered UoA 19 REF 2014 case studies. Interestingly, the average value of 'percent national reach' across the three clusters was 48.4%, 47.3%, and 67.7% for the top, middle, and bottom groupings, respectively. The reach produced by the top- and middle-clustered institutions therefore provided an approximately equal distribution of impact between national and international perspectives, whilst the bottom grouping tended more towards case studies with a national impact only. This latter finding may derive from post-1992 universities being more embedded in their local area and consequently, with fewer connections internationally.

In any case, a thorough reading of UoA 19 impact case studies,[7] clearly illustrates the extraordinary and varied geographical reach of UK HEIs. Consider four examples. First, in terms of significant national impact, Professor Barbara Townley (University of St Andrews) and colleagues provided the case study, 'Capitalising on creativity in the film and screen industry', which demonstrated linkages between research that addressed organisational, innovation, and investment issues in the creative industries – such as the adoption of digital business models – and the impact on specific firms (including raising investment for a number of new films) and the public body that supports them. Second, with impact on policymakers in the UK and EU, the University of Strathclyde case study, 'The role of women entrepreneurs in UK economic development', built on their research demonstrating that the key role women entrepreneurs can play in economic growth is hampered by undercapitalisation at firm inception and thereby provided the rationale for women's enterprise initiatives that obtained significant amounts of both private and public sector funding. Third, with impact in Ireland, South Africa and the UK on over a 1,000 small firms, researchers from the Centre for Research in Innovation Management (University of Brighton) showed in their case study, 'Profitnet programme', that research on peer-to-peer networks – where small firms can be mentored and actively share knowledge, issues, and solutions – benefits strategic thinking and problem-solving, whilst increasing underlying sales, customer interactions, turnover, and profitability. Finally, in a University of Central Lancashire case study entitled, 'Global microfinance: Fighting against poverty in developing countries', Professor Thankom Arun demonstrated the global impact (e.g. Ghana, India, Sri Lanka, South Africa) of research; e.g. showing the importance of micro-insurance in diminishing the precarity of poorer households.

The exceptional reach of UK HEIs can be further evidenced by considering the geographical distribution of *all* impact case studies submitted to REF 2014. Here each case study has been coded[8] by country (or countries) of impact, and then aggregated by continent, enabling us to provide an assessment of the overall diversity of geographical reach.

Figure 5.5 shows the number of case studies by impact location for UoA 19. Each continent (excepting Antarctica) is represented, with the most impacts occurring in Europe (46%), followed by Asia (18%), North America (13%), Oceania (11%), Africa (7%), and South America (5%). Interestingly, Figure 5.6 shows a not too dissimilar distribution for all UoAs with Europe (42%), North America (19%), Asia (17%), Oceania (11%), Africa (6%), and South America (4%).

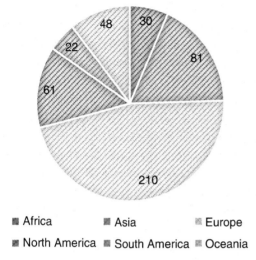

Figure 5.5 Number of case studies by impact location (UoA 19).

Notes: Source is https://impact.ref.ac.uk/casestudies/.

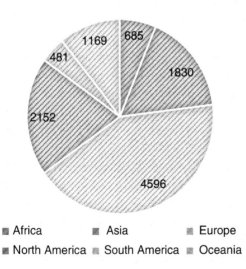

Figure 5.6 Number of case studies by impact location (all UoAs).

Notes: Source is https://impact.ref.ac.uk/casestudies/.

5.6   Conclusion

In this chapter, we have reflected on the UK REF2014 impact exercise in terms of the meso- and macro-level consequences of impact assessment for universities and business schools. To characterise the various intended and unintended consequences, we have coined four terms: the crowded-out university, the trapped university, the connected university, and the stretched university. As an audit mechanism, REF 2014 demonstrated that UK HEIs are producing excellent research-linked impact work, connected to both public and private sector organisations, and with a global reach. However, a burning question remains: is the exercise worth both the financial cost (estimated at £55m) and the 'impact' on universities and their staff?

To answer this question, we considered first the workload issue. The contemporary UK university is a crowded-out space, where overwork is common, and associated physical and mental health problems, rising. Targets and audit exercises, including the impact component of the REF, have been introduced with seemingly little thought as to consequences on workloads in general, or specifically, to the gendered distribution of tasks in the HEI sector. However, these consequences are very real. As one impact case study author in the Rand Europe (Manville et al., 2015a: 9) report stated: 'During the past year, I have written zero papers, I have not given the usual attention to gaining research funding and I believe that the process... has been disastrous for my research and potential, and potentially my own growing international reputation'.

In addition to the negative workload implications, the practice of audit in higher education leads inexorably to the production of league tables. Over the last twenty years, there has been a proliferation in the use of such rankings including *The Times* 'Good University Guide', the QS World University Rankings and the *Financial Times* (*FT*) Global MBA ranking, and universities assiduously target places. However, existing evidence (Wedlin, 2011) suggests that rankings can sustain the current status quo, effectively trapping universities – such as the UK post-1992 cohort – in a viewpoint that is transmitted globally.

Higher education is one of the most dynamic and important sectors in the UK; a sector, as we saw in Chapter 3, which contributes many billions of pounds to the UK economy and supports almost a million jobs. However, a picture is emerging of an *already successful* sector that is buckling under the imposition of targets and audits, with the ability to contest the existing university hierarchy becoming further inhibited. The REF impact assessment itself is a very partial 'accounting' exercise; only admitting a small proportion of the impact work undertaken by universities, with the actual impact of education and well as the research and knowledge transfer, several orders of magnitude higher. Before this sector is squeezed too tightly, there are important grounds to challenge both the existence and the operation of the exercise. Indeed, one could go further: there seems good cause to free universities from much of the target and audit burdens placed upon them; this will not only benefit universities themselves, but the people who work in them, the students they educate, and the positive social, cultural, and economic effects they generate.

Notes

1 see https://www.ref.ac.uk/2014/.
2 Impact case studies were awarded four stars (outstanding), three stars (very considerable), two stars (considerable), one star (recognised but modest), or unclassified (little or not eligible or not underpinned by excellent research) – see REF 02.2011: 44.
3 See https://www.ref.ac.uk/2014/media/ref/results/AverageProfile_All%20UOAs. pdf
4 Whilst the overall ranking of universities was produced using all inputs listed, subject rankings were derived from just four equally weighted inputs: research quality, student satisfaction, entry standards, and graduate prospects.
5 Of the 432 case studies submitted to REF, 2015 for UoA 19, 410 were available at https://impact.ref.ac.uk/casestudies/.
6 UoA 25 education presented 215 case studies, 176 of which were classified as education-research.
7 https://impact.ref.ac.uk/casestudies/
8 Again see https://impact.ref.ac.uk/casestudies/, where this coding has been carried out.

References

Aiston, S.J. and Jung, J. (2015) Women academics and research productivity: An international comparison. *Gender and Education*, 27 (3), 205–220.

Anderson, L., Ellwood, P. and Coleman, C. (2017) The impactful academic: Relational management education as an intervention for impact. *British Journal of Management*, 28 (1), 14–28.

Bourdieu, P. (1984) *Distinction: A social critique of the judgement of taste.* Cambridge, MA: Harvard University Press.

Equality Act (2010) https://www.legislation.gov.uk/ukpga/2010/15/contents. Accessed on 25 March 2021.

Erickson, M., Hanna, P. and Walker, C. (2020) The UK higher education senior management survey: a stataactivist response to managerialist governance. *Studies in Higher Education*, 1–18. Ahead-of-Print.

Fazackerley, A. (2019) It's cut-throat: Half of UK academics are stressed and 40% thinking of leaving. *The Guardian*, 21 May, https://www.theguardian.com/education/2019/may/21/cut-throat-half-academics-stressed-thinking-leaving. Accessed on 25 March 2021.

Green, S.E. (2004) A rhetorical theory of diffusion. *Academy of Management Review*, 29 (4), 653–669.

Green, S.E., Yuan, L. and Nohria, N. (2009) Suspended in self-spun webs of significance: A rhetorical model of institutionalization and institutionally embedded agency. *Academy of Management Journal*, 52 (1), 11–36.

Hall, R., and Bowles, K. (2016) Re-engineering higher education: The subsumption of academic labour and the exploitation of anxiety. Workplace: *A Journal for Academic Labor*, 28, 38–47.

Kellard, N.M. and Śliwa, M. (2016) Business and Management impact assessment in REF2014: Analysis and reflection. *British Journal of Management*, 27 (4), 693–711.

Lashuel, H.A. (2020) The busy lives of academics have hidden costs – and universities must take better care of their faculty members. *Nature*, 5 March, https://www.nature.com/articles/d41586-020-00661-w. Accessed on 25 March 2021.

Macfarlane, B. and Burg, D. (2019) Women professors and the academic housework trap. *Journal of Higher Education Policy and Management*, 41 (3), 262–274.

Manville, C., et al. (2015a) Preparing impact submissions for REF 2014: An evaluation (Findings and observations). *Rand Europe*. HEFCE.

Manville, C., et al. (2015b) Preparing impact submissions for REF 2014: An evaluation (Approach and evidence). *Rand Europe*. HEFCE.

Office of National Statistics (2019) Is staff retention an issue in the public sector? https://www.ons.gov.uk/economy/governmentpublicsectorandtaxes/publicspending/articles/isstaffretentionanissueinthepublicsector/2019-06-17. Accessed on 25 March 2021.

Ratle, O., et al. (2020) Mechanisms of micro-terror? Early career CMS academics' experiences of 'targets and terror' in contemporary business schools. *Management Learning*, 51 (4), 452–471.

REF (2011) REF 2014: assessment framework and guidance on submissions. https://www.ref.ac.uk/2014/pubs/2011-02/. Accessed on 25 March 2021.

REF (2015) Research Excellence Framework 2014: Overview report by Main Panel C and Sub-panels 16 to 26. https://www.ref.ac.uk/2014/media/ref/content/expanel/member/Main%20Panel%20C%20overview%20report.pdf. Accessed on 25 March 2021.

Ruth, D., et al. (2018) Anxious academics: Talking back to the audit culture through collegial, critical and creative autoethnography. *Culture and Organization*, 24 (2), 154–170.

The Times (2020) Good University Guide 2021 methodology: How we compiled the rankings. September 20, 2020. https://www.thetimes.co.uk/article/good-university-guide-2021-methodology-how-we-compiled-the-rankings-j5 63p2pn0. Accessed on 25 March 2021.

Wedlin, L. (2011) Going global: Rankings as rhetorical devices to construct an international field of management education. *Management Learning*, 42 (2), 199–218.

Wellcome (2020) What researchers think about the culture they work in. https://wellcome.org/reports/what-researchers-think-about-research-culture. Accessed on 16 March 2021.

Zucker, L.G. (1977) The role of institutionalization in cultural persistence. *American Sociological Review*, 42 (5), 726–743.

6　Putting impact to work

6.1 Introduction

In this final chapter, we first provide a synthesis of the argumentation presented in this book, and subsequently propose a series of recommendations with the aim of putting the impact agenda 'to work' for business schools across the world, so that it becomes 1) a vehicle for advancing business school contributions that are of highest societal value; 2) a channel through which business schools, as workplace organisations, can fulfil their objectives of building inclusive and sustainable organisational cultures.

Underpinning the recommendations stemming from our analysis is a view of HE as a successful sector that is part of the society, rather than one that influences it from the outside. Our recommendations are also underpinned by a conviction that it is important to understand the impacts that different activities which universities and business schools engage in – including those associated with impact generation and assessment – have on HEIs and the people working in them. Put differently: if the university sector, which, according to UUK (2017) supports close to a million jobs in the UK, is one in which inequalities and exclusions are perpetuated, and which is not in good health due to the multiple pressures it faces and the impacts these have on people's workloads, physical and mental health, and overall wellbeing, then this also means that inequalities and exclusions are perpetuated in society and that the society itself is not in good health. In light of this, the recommendations which we articulate below are guided by the need to put the good health and support for universities and business schools as a priority to which any audits, including impact assessments, ought to be subordinate. We have divided our discussion of recommendations into separate but interrelated sub-sections addressing specific stakeholder groups,

DOI: 10.4324/9781003090465-6

including: future research, HE policy-makers, university and business school leaders, and individual academics.

6.2 Synthesis of argumentation presented in this book

We began this book by drawing attention to the importance of the historical context in which the evolution of universities, and the business schools within them, has taken place, and the long-ongoing debates about the purpose and role of universities within society and economy. This contextualisation allowed us to highlight that thinking about universities in terms of their societal and economic usefulness – and being subject to state control and evaluation – did not always accompany the 'idea of the university', and that especially in the case of the UK, it was not until 1986 that the first national-level audit of universities' research performance, based on which funding was allocated to individual universities, was introduced. The historical contextualisation also enabled us to point to the emergence of management education in Britain in the 1960s, intended as a vehicle for educating a highly competent cadre of managers who would bring the performance of British organisations in line with those in Western Europe and North America, but not necessarily as a medium through which direct impacts on challenges faced by policymakers and industry leaders were to be generated. In the initial chapter of the book we also discussed the multiple types of societal and economic impacts which universities generate.

Subsequently, in the second chapter, we presented an overview of the literature addressing the impact and relevance of business and management research, summarising the key contributions to the so-called relevance debate. We pointed out that while a number of authors have contributed to the debate, and have suggested various solutions to the 'double hurdle' of academic rigour and practical relevance of BMS research, only a small proportion of existing literature addresses the scholar–practitioner relationship and the complexities of impact generation. We also highlighted some of the critiques of the impact agenda, e.g. with regard to how the desirability of impact seems to be taken for granted, who tends to be defined as 'practitioners', whose interests are prioritised for the purpose of impact generation, how impact activity is viewed by the academics engaged in it, and how the role of management education tends to be excluded from discussions of business schools' impact.

The third chapter elaborated on how research impact is framed by UK policymakers. In doing so, we focused on the UK government's policy framework for evaluating the quality of research conducted by HEIs, i.e. the Research Excellence Framework. We argued that although the idea of holding universities accountable for the way in which they use resources is understandable, the extent to which universities' activities are subject to external scrutiny suggests a distrust towards the HE sector. We located this distrust of universities within the broader context of suspicion towards 'experts', and connected it to the broader *Zeitgeist* of anti-intellectualism and populism. Following this background discussion, we examined the definition of impact as articulated within the UK's Research Excellence Frameworks (REF2014 and REF2021), and suggested that – having been developed from within the science disciplines – it might not provide an adequate way of capturing business schools' impact. Having compared the REF2014 and REF2021 guidance, we concluded that as far as impact assessment is concerned, only a fraction of the variety and import of UK business schools' impact is included in the assessment exercise.

The emphasis in the fourth chapter of the book was on the consequences of engagement in impact generation and assessment for different groups of academics and their careers. In particular, we argued that the ability to engage in impact is not diversity-neutral as it is unevenly distributed among researchers, with inequalities and exclusions affecting members of minority groups of staff such as early career researchers, women, and members of other minority groups. We highlighted the predominance of teamwork in generating impact and discussed the differences between the different groups of academics in terms of accessing both the academic networks through which impact generation takes place and the networks of stakeholders outside universities. Our argumentation also drew attention to the workload and career imbalances – which follow old patterns of gender inequalities – associated with impact generation.

Our analysis in the fifth chapter was driven by the question: is the REF impact assessment exercise worth both the financial cost (estimated at £55m during the REF2014 exercise) and the 'impact' on universities and their staff? In addressing it, we discussed a range of intended and unintended consequences of impact activity and assessment from a meso- and macro-level perspective, focusing on the effects on business schools, universities, society, and economy at the local, national, and international level. We emphasised both the benefits of the REF2014 impact process, such as a strategic and cultural shift towards an increased engagement of universities with external stakeholders, as well as its less positive aspects, such as the high cost involved in engagement in the REF impact process and the exclusion of certain types of impact from the REF audit. In particular, we high-lighted the opportunity costs and the negative consequences of engagement in impact activity and assessment, arguing that it crowds out other valuable activities that universities and business schools undertake, such as teaching, research, mentoring, and administration, and further contributes to the currently common but unsustainable culture and practice of overwork in academia, resulting in high levels of mental and physical health problems across the sector. Our analysis also drew attention to how the REF impact process in the UK has so far contributed to the perpetuation or even strengthening of structural divisions between HEIs in the UK. We have pointed out that since the REF profile of a university gets included in the construction of university league tables, such as *The Times* 'Good University Guide', and since only work classified by REF panels as 3* or 4* is given weighting, the REF scores ultimately do little to challenge the conventional orderings of HEIs in the business and management field. Finally, we argued that the REF process privileges certain types of business schools' research impacts – such as those that have an obvious 'fit' with the REF rules and those that are straightforward to evidence, for example, through obtaining testimonials – over others, such as those that might be seen as 'risky' due to the lack of clarity about how well they fall within the remit of the REF guidance, or ones where, e.g. for reasons of confidentiality, it is not easy to provide evidence linking research with impact.

6.3 Recommendations for future research

In the first instance, we call for further research that addresses the complexities and practicalities of generating impacts. As discussed earlier, existing literature has argued for making business and management research more relevant to management practice, e.g. through including impact in the design stage of a research project, and through an early engagement of practitioners in the research. However, more informative, empirical work – especially rich, insightful studies – is needed to build a fine-grained, comprehensive understanding of what it actually takes to produce research with impact.

Second, it is necessary to build a body of research that would help us understand the multifaceted impacts and consequences of impact activity and evaluation exercises on business schools, especially with regard to impacts on the schools' efforts in relation to equality, diversity, and inclusion. For example, in light of universities' legal obligation to comply with the Public Sector Equality Duty (part of the

Equality Act 2010), it would be informative to produce research evidence on the relationship between engagement in the generation and assessment of impact and business schools' ability to actively demonstrate due regard for advancing equality, specifically: 'removing or minimising disadvantages suffered by people due to their protected characteristics; taking steps to meet the needs of people from protected groups where these are different from the needs of other people; encouraging people from protected groups to participate in public life or in other activities where their participation is relatively low' (Equality and Human Rights Commission, 2021). We envisage that the work conducted in this line of research might combine studies that focus on each of the protected characteristics listed in the Equality Act 2010 separately, and also those conducted through an intersectional lens, since it has been shown that the most significant impacts in equality and inclusion terms can be found on the intersection of different categories of diversity (Nichols and Stahl, 2019).

Third, we would like to encourage accounting scholars to turn research attention to the costs of impact, and to develop frameworks that would allow us to better account for and understand the total costs for business schools and universities of impact activities and impact assessment exercises from a research-informed accounting perspective, that would involve consideration of full resource costing and therefore enable accounting for all costs that need to be dedicated by business schools to pursuing the impact agenda.

6.4 Policy recommendations

As our first policy recommendation, we would like to encourage policymakers to engage in greater reflexivity about the view of the higher education sector and the people who work within it that underpins HE policymaking. With regard to the former, we recommend that policymakers recognise more explicitly the fact that HE is a very successful sector that makes an extremely valuable and strong contribution to society and economy. Whilst it is possible to consider the impacts of each university separately, it might, indeed, be more productive to place a greater emphasis on acknowledging these impacts at the level of the entire sector. This approach to understanding HEIs' impact would pay more attention to consideration of sector- rather than university- or business school-level data, such as how many students the HE sector educates overall, how much it contributes to building the knowledge- and skills-base of the country, how many people it employs, and how much revenue it generates. It might lead to the conclusion that instead of focusing on putting universities in competition with one another, which is what global rankings such as QS encourage, and national-level audits such as REF and within it impact assessment exercises contribute to, it would be more beneficial for the society and economy to encourage collaboration among universities in a given national context.

With regard to the latter, we suggest that policymakers scrutinise assumptions about the people who work in HE. Based on our experience of over 20 years' employment in UK universities, we believe that those who work in HE are predominantly highly committed and trustworthy individuals. Career decisions behind the choice to become an academic remain to a large extent underpinned by a sense of vocation. Before someone gets appointed to an academic position, many years of education and training are necessary, and the outcome tends to be uncertain, as there are fewer academic jobs than candidates who would like to take them. For those fortunate enough to secure an academic position, the position itself is often, for a number of years, a precarious one, and even the so-called permanent academic jobs are in many national contexts, such as Australia and the UK, constantly subject to a realistic threat of redundancies. In addition, academic salaries are not very high compared to the remuneration in other professions such as law and accountancy, and in many countries the end of an academic career is not currently rewarded with a generous retirement pension. From our longstanding experience, individuals who are attracted to the academic career tend to choose this trajectory because they are passionate about knowledge and learning themselves, and about educating future generations.

Our next recommendation for HE policymakers is to also engage in reflexivity about the role that HE policymakers and policies play towards the university sector. We would suggest that, instead of primarily fulfilling the role of auditing and evaluating the activities of HEIs, policymakers adopt a stronger, explicit focus on fulfilling a supportive role. With more support, the already successful HE sector will be able to continue making a valuable contribution to society and economy. Having a clear view of themselves primarily as supporters of universities would have a range of implications for the policymakers' actions towards the sector. To begin with, it would bring about a recognition that, since the ubiquity of the excellence assessment rhetoric is underpinned by undertones of distrust, it results in a sense of being distrusted and disrespected, rather than supported, in those who work in universities. Further, it would necessitate establishing, a priori, whether any new assessment framework – including impact assessment – that the policymakers are considering for introduction is going to be supportive of the HE sector and the people working within it, and to ensure that audit frameworks which are likely to have exclusionary or detrimental effects on those they are designed to audit are not going to be introduced.

In a similar vein, the current set of audits would also need to be reviewed in a holistic way, with a view to deciding whether and how it might need to be modified – and possibly reduced – in order to bring about outcomes that will be supportive of the HE sector and its people, including those working in business schools. As we have discussed earlier, the impact measurement exercise currently in place as part of the REF audit in the UK results in exclusionary outcomes for minority groups, and has problematic consequences for individuals' workload and stress levels, and relatedly, for their health and wellbeing. This, in itself, provides a good basis for policymakers to question whether it should be maintained. Also important to state is that in the UK context, the REF exercise is only one of a number of audits – including the National Student Survey (NSS), the Teaching Excellence Framework (TEF), and possibly in the foreseeable future the Knowledge Excellence Framework (KEF), that universities are expected to adhere to simultaneously. In the case of business schools in particular, there are often also additional audits associated with participation in the international global market for management education, such as the Association of American Colleges and Schools of Business (AACSB), EQUIS, and Association of MBAs (AMBA) accreditations. In light of the existence of multiple audits and the range of problematic impacts they have on the HE sector and its people, we strongly recommend that HE policymakers constructively engage with the issue of what could be done about the current university auditing system in order to support HEIs in their societal mission; to help them improve their ability to pursue equality, diversity, and inclusivity; to prevent further deterioration of the mental and physical health of HE staff, and to stop the escalation of costs to universities of preparing audit submissions.

6.5 Recommendations for university and business school leaders

Our analysis also gives rise to several recommendations for university and business school leaders. First, there is a need for HE leaders to develop an in-depth awareness of the complex, multifaceted, and often unmeasured and unspoken implications and consequences of participation in impact generation activity as well as impact assessment exercises. As we have argued throughout this book, these implications go far beyond the institutional or business school ranking positions to which the outcome of the exercise contributes, and affect staff careers and wellbeing, as well as the institutions' and business schools' ability to fulfil a range of their objectives. There are, as we have shown in the analysis, tangible and unevenly distributed implications and consequences for different groups of staff, in that not everyone has the same capacity to engage in and benefit from impact generation, with inequalities associated with engagement in impact particularly strongly affecting members of minority groups. We recommend to HE leaders and, in particular, to business school leaders that they proactively build their own awareness of how hard their staff, including both academics and professional services employees, work in order to fulfil all the tasks and responsibilities placed upon them, and what impact this has on them.

Moreover, we recommend that – regardless of the significance placed upon audit initiatives by forces external to universities – HE and business school leaders remain conscious of the finite nature of the resources at their disposal, and of the fact that when attention is given to one area, other areas will suffer. As discussed in the book, the primary objective behind the establishment of business schools was the formation and training of highly competent managers who would contribute in a societally and economically beneficial to the management of organisations. With high student numbers and constantly evolving educational programmes to reflect the needs of contemporary organisations, the structures and operations of business schools continue to reflect this objective. At the same time, the primary purpose that lay at the foundation of business schools was *not* to solve the practical problems of industry or to influence national- or international-level policy, and the structures and resources at business schools' disposal do not typically reflect such a purpose. Therefore, even though – as a result of impact assessment requirements – business school academics are able to prove that they are capable of influencing management practice and policy, engagement in impact activity comes at the expense of focusing on educating students and furthering management knowledge through research.

One way of ensuring that impact generation for REF purposes does not prevent business school academics from making impact through educating future and current management practitioners and developing management knowledge, could be through allocating the task of industry and policy impact generation to dedicated, possibly cross-faculty, interdisciplinary teams of practice- and policy-oriented staff, rather than making it a requirement that, at least potentially, applies to all academics. We also recommend that university and business school leaders acknowledge to a greater extent the impact that business schools have on management practice through educating students, and that they adopt it as a principle that – should there be another REF audit and another impact assessment exercise – at least one impact case study should focus on the submitting business school's educational activity.

Alongside the development of awareness and knowledge, we also recommend to HE and business school leaders that they take steps towards building and strengthening collaboration mechanisms with other leaders in the sector. In the case of the UK, these mechanisms could involve making greater use of existing associations and structures such as the British Academy of Management (BAM), the Chartered Association of Business Schools (CABS), University and College Union (UCU), and Universities UK (UUK). Whilst the current emphasis on audits such as impact assessment puts universities in rivalry with one another, we recommend that HE and business school leaders do not internalise the competition imperative but, rather, come together to act in a collaborative spirit.

A stronger orientation towards collaboration among universities and business schools would create the basis for implementing another recommendation which we would like to put forward: namely, to use spaces such as BAM, CABS, UCU, and UUK to debate and contest the purposes, costs, and consequences of external audits, including the REF impact assessment. Engagement in collaborative debate and contestation will then make it possible to develop constructive opposition and collective resistance to such requirements where they are seen to be excessively costly and at the same time unsupportive of or even detrimental to HEIs and business schools, and those who work in them.

6.6 Recommendations for individual academics

We end our discussion of recommendations with brief suggestions for all business school academics, from early career researchers to leaders, bearing in mind that the latter are also subject to the impact agenda, rather than simply being in charge of implementing it 'from above'. Specifically, we call for colleagues in business schools not to internalise the imperative to always 'deliver performance' on all fronts: education, research, management, citizenship, and impact, and to be aware that fulfilling all these types demands is impossible without a high personal cost to one's ability to achieve work-life balance, to enjoy good health and wellbeing, and to have a reasonable level of satisfaction from work. Therefore, it is important for individual academics to make informed decisions about which activities are nurturing for one's personal and professional development, and therefore worth pursuing. It will also be helpful for all of us working in business schools to reflect on how the impact agenda is shaping our identities, our own sense of relevance as business and management academics, and the way in which we view others. Let us remember: as educators, throughout our careers, we prepare thousands of talented individuals for management roles in a range of organisational and geographical settings. As researchers, we contribute to building management knowledge and to continuously updating our own knowledge and skills. As such, in these two key academic roles, we already make a strong, positive impact on society and economy, and prove through our everyday work that we are highly relevant to management practice.

6.7 Implications for the international context

The argumentation presented in this book is relevant internationally, although the UK remains the country with the longest tradition of government audits of the quality of research produced by higher education institutions. Beyond the UK, Australia's first national research evaluation, the Excellence in Research for Australia (ERA) exercise for universities, took place in 2010 and then subsequently in 2012, 2015, and 2018.[1] Alongside this, an opening Engagement and Impact (EI) assessment first took place in 2018 with another scheduled for 2024.[2] This latter exercise is similar in scope to impact assessment in the UK REF with research impact being defined as 'the contribution that research makes to the economy, society, environment or culture, beyond the contribution to academic research' (Australian Research Council, 2018: 6). Subjects were similarly grouped in Units of Assessment (e.g. UoA 15 Commerce, Management, Tourism and Services is analogous to the UK's REF 2014 UoA 19 Business and Management Studies) with the assessment itself based separately on both impact case studies and engagement with research end users. This latter category has overlap with the Knowledge Exchange Framework[3] in the UK, with the Australian exercise defining research engagement as 'the interaction between researchers and research end-users outside of academia for the mutually beneficial transfer of knowledge, technologies, methods, or resources' (Australian Research Council, 2018: 6).

Given the similarities between Australian (ERA and EI) and UK (REF) exercises, several of the learning points we derive from the UK context, likely apply in the Australian situation. At the time of writing, the Australian Research Council (ARC) had recently carried out a review of their research exercises,[4] providing 22 recommendations (see ERA EI Review Advisory Committee, 2021) including, amongst other things, suggesting further work to 'develop an equitable and appropriate calculation methodology for the number of required impact case studies' (Recommendation 8) and 'that the ARC continue to monitor understandings of research excellence and investigate how they may be incorporated into future rounds of ERA and EI' (Recommendation 22). Given our work, we would suggest such recommendations go even further and seek explicitly to understand the likely differential burdens (and opportunities) for individual researchers, particularly those from minority groups.

There are other international settings where currently, research impact monitoring initiatives are less formalised but where thinking about the important role of impact, and the appropriate concomitant methodologies for assessment, is nonetheless taking place. For example, a position paper (Ministry of Business, Innovation and Employment, 2019) for the New Zealand Government offers an impact measurement framework in order to 'progress the research impact agenda in New Zealand' (p. 1) but recognises some of the inherent risks, highlighting that 'The technical challenges with measuring impact mean there is a risk of drawing incorrect conclusions or creating perverse incentives, such as encouraging applied research over basic research, rewarding good luck, or penalising researchers for factors beyond their control' (p. 2). Our book encourages the examination of such risks in more detail.

Aside from governments requiring evidence of the impact of research, increasingly, accrediting and professional bodies, including those within the ambit of business schools, are requiring an analogous approach. To take one example, the Association to Advance Collegiate Schools of Business (AACSB), brings together over 900 accredited schools across 58 countries including in Africa (e.g. Egypt, Nigeria, and South Africa), Asia (e.g. China, Indonesia, and Japan), and South America (e.g. Argentina, Brazil, and Colombia).[5] The recently revised 2020 business accreditation (AACSB, 2020), presents nine standards, of which two focus explicitly on impact; specifically Standard 8 covers the 'Impact of Scholarship' whilst Standard 9 examines 'Engagement and Societal Impact'. To evidence the meeting of these standards, in part, schools should employ 'qualitative and/or quantitative metrics, [and] provide an analysis of the impact made by the school's portfolio of intellectual contributions' (AACSB, 2020; p. 54). Whilst welcoming the emphasis on positive societal impact, accrediting bodies and their business school partners should be aware of the unintended consequences impact work can create. As a corollary, further iterations of such standards could include greater reference to workplace equality, inclusion, and workloads around impact generation.

6.8 Conclusion

As two academics with ample experience of education, research, and leadership in the UK business school context, we have written this book with a view to highlighting the 'impact of impact', exemplified by the unmeasured and usually unspoken about aspects and consequences of engagement in impact generation and the impact assessment exercise through the REF. Whilst we do not claim that all the lessons that can be learned from the British case for HEIs and business schools apply internationally, based on the available evidence, we believe that many of these lessons will be valid when other country contexts are considered. Local conditions inevitably vary and comparative research is needed to understand the different ways in which they do. At the same time, different contexts share similarities amongst themselves. For example, both in the UK and in other countries there is still a long way to go before inequalities and exclusions are overcome, and before academia becomes an inclusive sector; in many countries, academic jobs are increasingly uncertain, making ECRs' situation particularly precarious; workloads that are equally high or even higher than in the UK are not uncommon in HE internationally; and the work of academics across the world is subject to a range of performance evaluation audits, which are not necessarily supportive of people's work-life balance and physical and mental health. Likewise, all over the world, business school academics do a great job educating successive generations of managers, producing and developing of new knowledge, methodologies, and theoretical perspectives, disseminating scholarly research addressing all aspects of business and management, and contributing to the day-to-day and strategic running of the business schools and HEIs they work for. We therefore trust that the analysis and discussion presented in this book will be considered as informative and thought-provoking by academics, HE and business school leaders, and policymakers both within and outside the UK. It is our hope that we have articulated a set of valuable ideas that will enrich the debate on business schools' impact.

Notes

1 See https://www.arc.gov.au/excellence-research-australia
2 See https://www.arc.gov.au/engagement-and-impact-assessment
3 See KEF (2020).
4 See https://www.arc.gov.au/excellence-research-australia/era-ei-review
5 https://www.aacsb.edu/accreditation/accredited-schools

References

AACSB. (2020) 2020 Guiding Principles and Standards for Business Accreditation.

Australian Research Council. (2018) EI 2018 Assessment Handbook.

Equality Act (2010) https://www.legislation.gov.uk/ukpga/2010/15/contents. Accessed on 25 March 2021.

Equality and Human Rights Commission. (2021) Public Sector Equality Duty. https://www.equalityhumanrights.com/en/advice-and-guidance/public-sector-equality-duty. Accessed on 24 March 2021.

ERA EI Review Advisory Committee. (2021) ERA EI Review Final Report 2020–2021.

Knowledge Exchange Framework. (KEF, 2020) Decisions for the first iteration.

Ministry of Business, Innovation and Employment. (2019) The impact of Research. Position paper (October, 2019).

Nichols, S. and Stahl, G. (2019) Intersectionality in higher education research: A systematic literature review. *Higher Education Research and Development*, 38 (6), 1255–1268.

UUK (2017) Increasing impact of world-leading university sector on jobs and growth should not be 'taken for granted', warn university leaders. https://www.universitiesuk.ac.uk/news/Pages/economic-impact-uk-universities-taken-for-granted.aspx. Accessed on 24 March 2021.

Index